Mountains and Molehills

Mountains and Molehills

Questions For Christian Growth

Molly Dow

alpha

Copyright © 1997 Molly Dow
First published in Great Britain in 1997
by Triangle, SPCK

This edition published in 2000 by Alpha
06 05 04 03 02 01 00   7 6 5 4 3 2 1

Alpha is an imprint of Paternoster Publishing,
PO Box 300, Carlisle, Cumbria, CA3 0QS, UK
and PO Box 1047, Waynesboro, GA 30830-2047, USA
www.paternoster-publishing.com

British Library Cataloguing in Publication Data

A catalogue record for this book is available from
the British Library

ISBN 1-898938-02-4

Scripture quotations are taken from the
NEW REVISED STANDARD VERSION BIBLE,
copyright 1989, Division of Christian Education of
the National Council of the Churches of Christ in
the United States of America. Used by permission.
All rights reserved

Cover design by Diane Bainbridge
Printed in Great Britain by Cox & Wyman
Cardiff Road, Reading, Berkshire, RG1 8EX

Contents

Molly Dow has a degree in Chemistry from Oxford University; she also holds a Diploma in Theology and has been a Reader in the Church of England for many years. She is married to Graham, the Bishop of Carlisle, and is the mother of four adult children. She has studied Ignatian spirituality and has been involved in giving spiritual direction. She was the Spirituality Adviser for the Willesden Area of the Diocese of London, where she also co-produced various courses on personal and corporate prayer.

Acknowledgements

I am very grateful to Keith Danby, Rob Cook and all at Paternoster Publishing who have been so helpful in producing this commemorative edition in time for my husband's enthronement as Bishop of Carlisle. My thanks go to him, too, for writing a foreword at a time of unpacking after our move and preparing for the beginning of an important new ministry.

Many people have contributed to this book in seen or unseen ways. 'Thank you' to those who have helped me over the years with my mountains and molehills, to those who have shared something of their own journeys with me and to those who have given me help and encouragement in my writing.

Foreword

This book, first published in 1997 is kindly being reissued by Paternoster Publishing in order to commemorate the start of the ministry that Molly and I will have in Cumbria. We are immensely grateful for such support.

I do not think that the publishers will be disappointed. My wife's book is about the kind of questions that we all have, sometimes even the questions that we are afraid to voice. The chapter headings tell the story: 'Will God grow tired of forgiving me?'; 'What if God discovers how bad I really am?'; 'How can I cope when God seems absent?'; 'What is the meaning of life?' Travelling round the parishes in London I have only needed to read out some of the chapter titles and straight away people wanted copies of the book.

Of course, I am one of my wife's chief fans. Yet the book is as good as the chapter headings suggest. Molly has an inquiring mind which will not leave difficult issues alone. She wants to know the truth. From the scriptures and from her own experience she faces the difficulties in the journey of faith and offers the insights and directions that she has found helpful over the years. As the Archbishop of York wrote in his foreword to the 1997 edition, 'it is an immensely encouraging book'.

The book makes an ideal Confirmation gift for a thoughtful candidate. It is practical, readable and addresses those questions on the journey of faith that come into the minds of us all. It is also a good book to take away on a retreat. My hope is that it will provide light on the journey for many people in our churches who are looking for help in the ups and downs of being a Christian today.

Each chapter concludes with a prayer. This helps to draw heart and mind together. It clearly expresses our dependence upon God. Through thought and prayer together our faith grows.

Graham Dow
Bishop of Carlisle

Introduction

In this book I want to share some of the ways in which God has helped me to move forward with him, in spite of the many obstacles in my path. Some have seemed like mountains, others no more than molehills. I suspect that sometimes I have made mountains out of what need only have been molehills.

I have shared much of the material of this book already, in sermons, group discussions and personal conversations. People's responses seem to indicate that many of the questions and struggles I have had to work through are not mine alone. The ways in which God has helped me have proved helpful to others also.

Each person's situation is unique, and God's gifts and help are personal – I do not claim to have found *the* answers for everyone. I still have a lot to learn, and there are many other helpful approaches to these questions. There is, after all, more than one way to get past a molehill, or over a mountain.

In my experience, other people's solutions to problems cannot always be lifted as they are and applied to our own situations to produce an instant remedy. We have to work at them to make them our own. We have to try them on for size, and ask God what alterations must be made before they fit us and our needs.

Each of us brings a different personality and set of circumstances to any question. Our lives and all around us are interdependent in so many complex ways, and only God can take everything into account, for he is our maker and knows all the secrets of our hearts. He alone knows what we can cope with and what is the very best for us; one person's mountain is another person's molehill.

1

How can I cope when God seems absent?

It is hard, when you have come to value God's love and friendship, to lose the sense of his presence and his caring for you. Yet it is common for Christians to experience such bleak 'desert' times, when prayer can be difficult and dry. It may simply be that God seems distant and we wonder if he is really listening or doing anything to help. But sometimes it is only a small step from saying that God *feels* far away to saying that he is actually absent: we may then even doubt whether he exists at all. The questioning, doubt and sense of desolation can be very painful. Experience tells us, however, that these times do not last for ever, that they have value and that there are ways we can help ourselves through them.

One of my toughest desert experiences did coincide with a time of doubt. During my second year at university, I had an inner crisis, doubting almost everything about the Christian faith. I asked, 'Does God exist? If he does, does he care about me? Is he the sort of personal being that Christians say he is? Are the Gospels reliable accounts of Jesus' life and teaching? Did Jesus really rise from the dead? … and so on, and so on.

I began to wonder if I only believed in Jesus because of my Christian background, or because I wanted to believe, rather than because I was fully convinced that his life and teachings were true. Had I thought things through honestly or deeply enough? Was I prepared to face the possiblity that I had been kidding myself?

I felt very alone. It was awful to think that there might be no God. I had been a Christian for several years, since my early teens, and my relationship with God was very important to me. He was the only person who really understood me through and through. If he did not exist, what had been going on at those times when I thought I was experiencing him? And if he was not there, there was no one utterly reliable to take me safely through life and death. Perhaps, if I could be *absolutely sure* that there was no God, it might not be too bad: I would still be alone, but I could at least live as I liked, with no fear of eventual judgement! But I reckoned that belief in no God at all requires at least as much faith as belief in God's existence.

I was afraid of persuading myself into faith, just because I *wanted* to believe. More than anything, I wanted to know the truth and to follow it, whatever it was, whether it turned out to be God or not. Yet I didn't see how I could ever be sure of where the truth lay.

So what did I do? And how, if at all, did it help? Well, I cried a lot – to God, if he was there! And I prayed. My prayers were mostly in the form of, 'God, if you're there, *help!*'. Although I wasn't sure whether or not he was there, I thought that if he was there, and if he was at all nice or good, if he was interested in human beings at all, he would *have* to answer somehow, sometime. It would be unreasonable and unjust of him not to.

I also read a lot – all the books I could find which dealt with the question 'Is it true?' – and I thought long and hard about what I was reading. Eventually, I came to the conclusion that many others had reached before me: that it is impossible to prove the existence of God beyond any shadow of doubt. Nor could you prove scientifically (and I was a scientist, studying chemistry) any historical fact, including the facts of the life, death and resurrection of Jesus. There could always be an alternative theory as to what happened, so the sort of proof I wanted, of the existence of God and of the resurrection of Jesus, was unobtainable.

This turned out to be quite helpful, because I came to the conclusion that the Christian understanding of God and Jesus was at least reasonable, and maybe even probable. It wasn't the end of the road, because I then had to decide whether or not I was prepared to commit my whole life to someone or something that was only probable and not provable. Still, I had made some progress: I had a reasonable basis for a give-it-a-try approach to Christian faith.

And I talked to a few people. I can remember two helpful things that were said to me. The first was to avoid cutting myself off from Christian fellowship and worship, since that was one of God's most likely ways of getting through to me. I followed this advice, although it was very hard to sit through services and meetings where people were saying, praying and singing things I wasn't sure I believed. It didn't help me back to faith, as far as I know, but it did mean that when my faith was rekindled, I didn't have to make a self-conscious return to a Christian community.

The second thing, and the most helpful, was being directed to Deuteronomy 8:2, which speaks of God using the Israelites' 40 years in the wilderness to show whether or not they really wanted to follow him. 'God has led you in the wilderness [or desert] … to *know what was in your heart.'* The very bleakness of my experiences gave me a chance to show God that I loved him for his sake, not only for my own sake. Following God can feel very worthwhile when our lives are going smoothly and our faith brings us peace, joy, friends, comfort and other good things. We love God and want to serve him because of what we receive. But following God when things are difficult, when we seem to receive only suffering and hardship, is rather different. It gives us an opportunity to show him a love that has a minimum of self-interest abut it. And that was what I wanted to do. So I tried to worship and pray and to run my life as I believed God wanted. I wasn't sure what I expected to happen, or whether I would ever again come to a position of confident faith, but I was prepared to stick at it for God's sake.

If Christianity were true, I hoped to see such things as love and goodness growing in my life and the lives of Christians in general. I also expected to see good things happening in other people's lives in answer to my prayers. If, on the other hand, there was no God and Jesus did not rise from the dead, I expected to discover that Christians showed no more growth in love and goodness than other people, and that prayers were not answered.

As I came out of my desolate time of doubt, I realized that several good things had come out of it. First, I was glad to have discovered that when I cast myself on God's goodness, as honestly and openly as I knew how, he did not let me down: I emerged with a Christian faith that was stronger, not weaker, than before.

Also, investigating the evidence for God's existence and Jesus' resurrection had been very worthwhile, and had given my faith a surer foundation, resting on a probability that was reasonable, rather than an unjustifiable claim to proof.

Another benefit was the sense not only that God was with me now, but that he had been there all along, although I had not been aware of him. It is ultimately more important that he actually is there, than that I can know his presence or feel that he is there.

I was really grateful, too, for having been shown Deuteronomy 8:2, because through it, I came to see that hard experiences can be great opportunities to learn from God and to grow.

And lastly, I was pleased to have had a chance to discover and then to show, to myself and to God, that I don't only love him for what I get from him, but also for himself alone.

I once watched a television interview with M. Scott Peck, the American psychiatrist who is also a Christian, in which he said that everything that happens in our lives - but especially the hard things - provides us with an opportunity to learn. I agree very much with him, and think that my experience of doubt was just one illustration of that. The desert was unpleasant, but I am glad of it: for the ways in which I learned and grew through it, and for all that I discovered about myself and about God. I thank God that he 'led [me] in the wilderness ... to know what was in [my] heart'.

With the benefit of a few more desert times of various kinds over the years, I have drawn up some survival tactics.

- **Check for 'natural causes'.** Sometimes the reason for a dry time spiritually lies in our circumstances. If we are unwell or tired, the whole of our life is affected, including our relationship with God. The same applies when we are bereaved, or suffering from other kinds of loss and stress. Then we need to take care to be kind to ourselves.
- **Keep in touch with God.** This means being open and honest with God about what we are thinking, feeling and wanting. God wants to deal with us as we really are. Our prayers are likely to be short and to the point. In addition to 'God if you're there, help!' I have prayed things like:

  'Why don't you do something?'
  'Lord, help me to trust you.'
  'Help me to keep going.'
  'I've had enough!'

Familiar prayers we know by heart, such as the Lord's Prayer and the Jesus Prayer ('Lord Jesus Christ, have mercy on me') can also be helpful.

● **Keep in touch with Christian people.** I have mentioned already the value of not cutting ourselves off from worship and the Christian community.

● **Concentrate on thanksgiving.** However little we may feel like giving thanks, to remind ourselves of God's goodness and many gifts to us builds faith. It is good to be as specific as possible. Some Psalms and hymns can be helpful when we are stuck for our own words. Knowing that others have felt dry and desolate too can be comforting.

It is also helpful to thank God for whatever good he will bring out of the time of difficulty. We don't have to pretend that the difficulty itself is good when it isn't.

● **Hang on in there.** We do well to trust God to bring us through. Desert experiences are quite common and they do come to an end. We should try to be patient and hopeful.

● **Look upwards and outwards.** Although it may seem at times that our desert is all there is, this is obviously not true. Making the effort to concentrate more on God and on other people will help us to see things in better perspective. It is also part of seeking to love God for his sake, rather than ours.

- **A trouble shared is a trouble halved.** Telling one or two trusted Christian friends what we are going through and asking them to pray for us can be very supportive.
- **Turn to your basic rations.** Go to familiar verses and passages of Scripture that you know and love. Read them, repeat them by heart, if possible, letting them comfort and strengthen you. You do not have to work at them, merely allow them to be there alongside you as friends. I once heard Cardinal Basil Hume say, 'Make friends among the Psalms'. There are Psalms to meet many different moods, and it is good to be able to find our own favourites when we need them. Favourite hymns, poetry and books can be sustaining too, especially when they show us that someone else has felt similarly. They help us to feel understood, and therefore less isolated.

A meditation

Meet me in the desert, Lord

How did I get here?
I thought you were with me, guiding me.
Where are you?
Did I mistake your voice?

I used to think I heard you, felt your touch …
    But now?
Have I gone deaf, or are you silent?
Do you really mean me to be here,
Or have I taken a wrong turning?
I'm lost without you.
Meet me in this desert, Lord,
And show me where I'm meant to be.

Emptiness and wasteland,
Dry and dusty, barren.
No protection from the sun,
No satisfaction for my hunger and my thirst.
I see no end, no hope and no way out of here.
I'm helpless.
Yet there are signs that others have been here
    before me.
Was their journey through this desert a mistake,
Or the best route to where you wanted them
    to be?
Were they wandering aimlessly, bereft,
Or were you leading them?
And I, am I bereft,
Or are you watching over me?
Then meet me in this desert, Lord,
And lead me out of here.

Come and get me out of here.
I'm tired of going this way.
I've had enough.
The desert just goes on and on.

I've had enough, I said.
Why don't you come?
Do you know how I feel, and do you care?
… I think you do.
I hunger and I thirst, but I'm not dying.
Are you sustaining me in ways I do not know?
I have a sense that all may still be well,
That things are going on which I can't see.
May there be more to this terrain than meets
    the eye?
Are there streams underground,
Awakening life and growth within this desert?
And in me?
A hidden work, deep and invisible,
If this is where you want to deal with me,
To bring your life and growth,
Then, 'Thank you, Lord'.
And I will stay here with you, for as long as
    you decide.
Meet me in this desert, Lord.
And lead me where you will.

2

Can Jesus really satisfy me?

'What do you want?' is a question we often hear in various circumstances, and our answers vary from the mundane to the deeply significant: 'I want fish and chips'; 'I want a new job'; 'I want to be known and loved'.

St Augustine said that our hearts are restless until they find their rest in God. Others, too, have spoken of deep inner longings, which the things of this world do not satisfy. We may sometimes get brief 'tasters' in special experiences of beauty, love, joy or wonder, but the pain of unsatisfied longing remains.

What do we really want? It is easy to think of things that people want for a satisfying life – health, happiness, friends, intimacy, fun, security, or a sense of purpose in life. Does ultimate satisfaction lie here, or are there bigger, deeper, more underlying things? If so, how can we discover what they are?

One way of discovering what is most important to us is to imagine God offering us one wish. What would our one wish be (not allowing the cheating wish to have all our other wishes granted)? When we think of that one wish, we try to imagine how life would be if that wish were granted. Would there be anything else that we would want? If so, we may not have discovered what we really want most.

We may discover various deep desires, sometimes overlapping, to do with our own needs and other people's. Some are personal, individual, while some are large-scale, concerning all humanity, the world and God. We may find we want to be known and understood, to love and be loved, or to know that we matter, that our lives are of value and significance. We may express this in biblical terms of evil being judged and destroyed, suffering coming to an end and all tears being wiped away. We may use words like forgiveness, reconciliation and harmony throughout creation. We may desire something that will last forever, beyond death – such as truth, love, goodness, justice. Or it may be something breathtaking and indescribable, for which we cannot even find words. C.S. Lewis called it 'joy', while Michael Mayne, Dean of Westminster, calls it 'wonder'.

If we want to express this indescribable desire in explicitly Christian terms, we might call it a desire for God, for being at one with him. Or we might say we are longing for the Kingdom of God, when God reigns completely and everything is as he wants it to be, full of love and justice, with no evil or suffering. Perhaps all longing for what is good is ultimately a desire for God himself, even when we do not recognize it as such.

This desire for 'something more' has been part of me for as long as I can remember, so I have always been intrigued by Jesus' words in John 4:14: 'Those who drink of the water that I will give them will never be thirsty.' What did he mean? Is Jesus offering to meet our deepest longings? Can we trust him to satisfy them fully?

Thirsty for goodness, truth and love

I believe many Christians find that Jesus himself does satisfy deep needs and longings, but that nobody feels completely satisfied all the time. Eventually they are thirsty again.

We thirst for goodness. We may have discovered that Jesus showed us perfect goodness in his own life. We may also have discovered that he 'clothes' us in his goodness, so that we can have relationship with God. We may even have found that, by trusting him and welcoming his Holy Spirit into our lives, goodness is growing in us too. All this can make us glad and grateful, satisfied that we need not look elsewhere for goodness. Yet, at the same time, we also start to see more clearly how far short we still fall of God's standard of goodness – and so we want more. And we long to see goodness in the way all people treat each other in families and local communities, in national life and international relationships, all over the world.

We are thirsty for truth. We may have discovered that we can know God through Jesus, 'the Way, the Truth and the Life', but we are only too aware of how imperfectly we know and understand him. We do see truth in God and in Jesus, but, as yet, we know we cannot take it in fully.

We are thirsty for love. As with our thirst for truth and goodness, we see perfect love in Jesus, especially when we contemplate his dying for us. We receive perfect love from God through Jesus, although we do not always recognize or appreciate it. We have to receive God's love by faith, rather than through our senses – and this makes it harder at times to know what it is like, to be sure that it is really there. If we could look into Jesus' eyes to *see* his look of love, if we could *hear* his voice and *feel* his touch, we would be more sure of his love and thus more satisfied with it. We receive other people's love, and he gives us increasing love *for* others too – but this very increase makes us painfully aware of how far short we fall of perfect love, and we have to come back again and again to ask for more.

In our times of thirsting for goodness, truth and love, is it that Jesus has failed to satisfy, or is it that we have not allowed him to lead us into ways that would have satisfied us more? Or might it be that such times are an essential part of the journey towards full and ultimate satisfaction in him?

Sometimes it seems that Jesus satisfies our spirit so deeply that we do not feel a lack of anything else. This can happen even when our outward circumstances are very difficult. Yet at other times we do not feel that God's love is enough, because we cannot see, or hear, or touch him. We want to be held, touched and spoken to, to know that someone cares about us. And this is surely not a failing, or a sin, but part of what it means to be human. Jesus, too, has been a human being. He needed to have his physical and emotional needs met. He, too, needed human friendship and tangible love, as well as the love of his Father. This came home to me once when meditating on Matthew's account of Jesus' time praying in Gethsemane before his arrest. Jesus tells Peter, James and John that he is deeply distressed and asks them to stay awake with him. He

needs their friendship, their company. He
wants to know that they are there with him,
supporting and caring. If it was all right for
Jesus, who had a *perfect* relationship with God
the Father, to want and need people as well, it
is all right for us. It is not sinful – simply part
of being human.

There are periods in our lives when we do
feel satisfied with what Jesus gives us. We are
inwardly peaceful and content, perhaps with a
sense of deep joy and of being at one with
God. Then, after a time, we become less content, less satisfied again, not because of any
conscious difficulty or sin, but actually
because we long for more of God again.

One way of looking at this situation is to say
that, having been filled by God, our capacity
for him becomes enlarged, so there are now
more 'spaces' to be filled. It is like a balloon
being filled with water. The water stretches the
rubber of the balloon, so the balloon is no
longer full and needs more water to fill it completely. As we grow spiritually, we seek more
of God, more goodness, more faith, more love.

Another way of seeing it is to say that we
can never be completely filled with God in this
life. Our longing is for the infinite and
absolute, but our capacity to receive him, is
finite, in fact quite small. Nevertheless, the
more we know him the more we want to know
him. Thus, as we grow there is a repeating

cycle of seeking more of God, receiving more, delighting in what he gives and wanting him even more.

While we do not experience feelings of satisfaction all the time, we can always be satisfied in the sense that we know we are looking in the right direction for what matters most to us. Jesus can and will meet our deepest needs and longings. We have no need to look elsewhere. Jesus said to his disciples on one occasion when some of his followers were giving up, 'Do you also wish to go away?' Simon Peter's reply was, 'Lord, to whom can we go? You have the words of eternal life' (John 6:67-8). Peter was satisfied that he was looking to the right person for eternal life, to the one who could actually give it. The fullest possible satisfaction is there in Jesus, but our capacity continues to increase and our longings continue to give us pangs, until in heaven God enables us to receive all that he wants to give us.

A prayer

Loving Father, thank you that you know and understand the deepest longings of our hearts. Help us to rejoice in what we have already found in you, and keep us looking forward, reaching out to know you better and to bring in your reign of goodness, love and peace, when everyone's needs will be satisfied; through Jesus Christ, our Lord. Amen.

3

What is the meaning of life?

Does life have meaning, or is it pointless? What gives our lives significance and importance? What does God intend us to do with our lives?

Many of us ask questions like these, consciously or unconsciously, at certain stages of our lives. Such questions are often particularly important in adolescence, when we begin to make our own choices about our values in life, about where we will direct our energies, what work we will do. When we start a family, too, we wonder about the potential of the new lives we have brought into the world. And in middle-age, where I am now, we reflect on what we have done with life so far, which of our ambitions have been achieved and which will never now be realized. What is the meaning of the second half of life, as we think ahead to growing old and to death? The cycle of human life – birth, growing up, learning, working, ageing and dying – what is it all for?

What is the meaning of life for people starving to death in Africa, or for children with AIDS in Romania? What is the meaning of life for someone who has already achieved all their ambitions, or for someone who has no ambitions? What is the meaning of life for those serving life-sentences in prison? For someone married to a violent alcoholic?

If God has a general meaning for everyone's life, then it has to be a meaning relevant to everyone, whatever their situation. It has to be relevant to the very clever as well as those with severe mental disabilities, to the rich as well as the poor, both the healthy and the sick, the old and the young, the 'successful' and the 'unsuccessful'. It must also apply to people who have made mistakes and wrong choices, and ended up in unsuitable jobs or difficult marriages – or in any situation where they   are unhappy or frustrated. If there is a basic meaning to life, it must apply equally to us all.

I would expect it also to be something that is self-evidently worthwhile. As a Christian, I believe that it has to be a meaning that fits in with what God has revealed of himself and his purposes for the world.

Learning to love

There are many possible starting-points from which we might discover God's meaning for life, but I started with the question, 'What can we be or do in this life which will continue into eternity?' And the answer, I believe, is *learning to love*. I do not mean any of the more limited senses of that word, like sexual love, sentimental love, friendship or affection, good though these are. I mean the kind of love the New Testament describes as *agape*, in which we want the very best for others, and give ourselves, sacrificially if necessary, to bring that about.

One passage of Scripture which supports this is 1 Corinthians 13, the well-known chapter about love, which is often read at weddings. This chapter says plenty about the value of love in this life, even stating that several worthy qualities and gifts are of little value without love. It sets before us challenging standards of perfect love, and the last part of the chapter tells us that, although other things will pass away when this world ends, love never ends: it will continue into eternity.

This gives us a clue as to why love is so worthwhile; it is the essential nature of God and of his rule (the Kingdom of God), which has begun now and which will be complete in the next life. When love reigns everywhere, everything will be in harmony and peace, everyone's needs will be met, all tears will be wiped away and there will be fullness of joy and well-being for all.

When Jesus was asked which was God's greatest, or most important, commandment, he replied in terms of love. He said there were two great commands, or perhaps one command in two parts: 'love the Lord your God with all your heart, and with all your soul, and with all your mind, and with all your strength' and 'love your neighbour as yourself' (Mark 12:29-31). Love, then, is the most important guiding principle in our lives: we are to love God with all our being and to love other people as much as we love ourselves. Since none of us comes remotely near this when we start out in life, it must be very important, from God's point of view, that we spend our lives learning to do it better and better. In heaven, when we are purged of all self-centredness, we shall manage it perfectly.

So the idea that learning to love is God's meaning or purpose for our lives does seem to fit with Scripture. But are there any people for whom it is impossible to learn to love? If there are, how could this be God's purpose in life for everyone? For the most part, improving our loving does not depend on our outward circumstances, whether we are rich or poor, with or without work, successful or unsuccessful,

clever or not-so-bright. It doesn't even depend
on whether our life is spent with other people
or alone – although if alone, our loving of
other people might only be expressed in such
ways as praying for them, or writing letters, or
some other distance-method.

Receiving love

But what about those who, because of extreme
age or youth, or certain kinds of ill-health,
such as being in a coma, or a permanent vege-
tative state, are not aware enough of their sur-
roundings to be able to become more loving at
present?

While somebody in a very dependent state –
in a coma, for example – may not be able to
give much love, or learn how to give more
love, they can receive love, thereby giving
other people a great opportunity to express
love and to learn how to love better. For us
to learn to love others, there must be people
to receive our love. Those who cannot give
much love, by reason of their extreme disabil-
ity, or whatever, can still be right at the centre
of God's purposes by receiving love from others. And, of course, many disabilities are no
disadvantage at all from the point of view of
giving love. We can see, from the writings of
Jean Vanier and others, that severely disabled
people sometimes give love more generously

and unconditionally than those of us who seem to be more whole.

In some extreme situations we have discovered a general truth: that receiving love is as much part of the meaning of life as giving it. We should not look on receiving love as an unimportant, or less worthy part of the process. If God's purposes were to work out ideally, we would surely all be giving and receiving love continually.

It is not only in the extremes of age or illness that we may find it hard to learn to love other people. There are times when it seems that all those around us are against us, and the whole of life is a struggle, when it is hard even to *want* to give love, let alone to manage it! Or there may be certain individuals whom we find almost impossible to love, tempting us to concentrate on loving God and not bother about loving others. But God tells us that if we love him, we must love other people too. It may be very hard to love when in prison or oppressed, when our lives are restricted or under the control of others who make difficulties for us, when we come up against people whom we can't stand – but surely even at these times it is not *impossible* to learn to love, only a greater challenge – and all the more wonderful when we are able to do it.

It is very difficult, if not impossible, however, to give love if we have not previously received it. When people find it hard to give any love at all, they are usually suffering from a lack or distortion of the love given to them. Perhaps they have picked up the message that love has to be earned, so they cannot give it freely, without strings attached. Perhaps they have never seen anything recognizable as love, so they do not know how to do it. Perhaps they fear that if they give themselves in love, there may be nothing of themselves left. If then, God's meaning for life is connected with love, it cannot only be about learning to give it, but also about coming to experience it, learning to recognize it and welcome it.

So perhaps we need to expand our summary of God's purpose for our lives: rather than simply learning to love, we need to think of growing into love.

It is possible for anyone, Christian or not, to believe that growing into love is the meaning of life. It is also not necessary to be a Christian to love, or to grow in love. At some point, however, everyone comes to realize that they would like to give and receive love more fully than they can actually manage. We cannot, solely by our own efforts, fulfil completely the meaning and purpose of our lives.

Perfect love

How and where can we see perfect love so that we can model ourselves on it? If we are disabled in our loving by the damage and gaps in love we have experienced in the past, how can this be put right? If we all need to receive love in order to be able to give it, and if we do not have enough in ourselves, where can we find an unending supply of love?

The answer to all these questions is to be found in God through Jesus Christ.

The Bible tells us that God is love (1 John 4:16). The one infinite and perfect Being, he alone is infinite and perfect love. Therefore, to see perfect love we have to look at God. We can know something of God and his character from how he has revealed himself in the Old Testament, but we see him most clearly in Jesus. Jesus was God coming to live as a human being, showing us how perfect love can be expressed in human life. He showed us perfect love in the form in which we are best able to recognize and appreciate it.

He showed us God's love supremely by being willing to die for us, in order to reconcile us to God. He made it possible for us to be given a new start in a relationship with God. He has dealt with sin from our past which debilitates us, and has put us in touch with God and his perfect and infinite love, so that our damage can be healed. He gives us his love, making up for the love we lack.

He gives us his Spirit to live in us and strengthen us, a never-ending source of love to

give out to others, not only to the individuals
we meet in our daily lives, and to those who
benefit from the work we do, but also on a
larger scale; working for justice and the right-
ing of social wrongs; giving time, effort and
money to relieve suffering elsewhere in the
world.

We shall not grow into love instantly or
fully in this life. It is a process begun here and
perfected when Christ takes us through death
into eternal life with him. Nevertheless, seeing
this as the meaning of our lives gives us a
vision of something infinitely worthwhile. I
find it helps to keep me from discouragement,
when life seems hard and disappointing, or
when I have made a mess of things. There is
still something worthwhile to do and to go on
working at, and I find ways of doing this every
day, even if only in small ways.

A prayer

Thank you, Father, that you give meaning and
purpose to life. Help us to spend our lives growing into love, in whatever situation we may be.
When life seems difficult, humdrum or pointless, and when we have made mistakes, help us
to hang on to this vision and this hope; for Jesus'
sake. Amen.

4

How can I help my faith to grow?

Have you ever thought, 'I wish I had more faith', or, 'I wish my faith were stronger'? Many Christians have thought like this from time to time, or have heard other people say such things. But need any of us remain stuck with the level (and feebleness?) of faith we may have at present? Surely we are not merely passive recipients of whatever sized dollop of faith we happen to have? Yet, if we have some responsibility for the strength of our faith, how can we help it to grow?

Although we know that faith can grow and that our trust in God is not as strong as it could be, we may not be bothered by this much of the time. We muddle on, ignoring it and hiding behind other people's faith when necessary. Sometimes we may be aware that we do not really trust God enough to let him

have complete control over the whole of our
lives: our time, our priorities, our lifestyle, our
money and our relationships, for example. It
may be true, also, that we have fears, that we
are troubled by worries which do not fit well
with a life of faith. However, we can comfort
ourselves by thinking that there are other
Christians who seem to be like this too. So
although we may be wistful, from time to time,
about having a stronger faith, we get by, pushing the weakness of our faith to the back of our
minds – until we meet a crisis.

A crisis is often the time when we discover the true character and strength of our
faith. The crisis may be over relationships,
money, job, family, illness, accident, death –
or anything else that is important to us. We
may discover that our security really lies
in something other than God. Perhaps our
faith has been more like an optional extra, or a
game we have been playing, than a relationship of deep trust in someone around whom
the whole of life revolves. We end up feeling   not only worried and afraid, but also
ashamed because of the weakness of our trust
in God.

This can seem devastating, but it is not all
bad news, because it gives our faith an opportunity to grow – and we can thank God for
that. Crises have value, if they shake us out of
complacency.

Belief and trust

Before looking at how faith actually grows, we must remember that there are two main constituents of faith: believing and trusting.

- **Believing** has more to do with our minds and what we recognize as true about God: the fact that he exists, what he is like, what he has done for us and what he does now.
- **Trusting** is more personal: it is our own response to God. It is the extent to which we put ourselves in his hands, confident that he is trustworthy and will do the best with us and for us. It is like a child jumping off a wall into her father's arms: the child chooses to jump, because she trusts her father to catch her.

We could say that the believing side of faith is concerned with what we take in: our taking on-board the truth about God, his goodwill towards us and what this has led him to do. The trusting side of faith, however, involves a more outward movement: we reach out our hand and put it into the hand of God, which is already extended towards us. We give, we love, we dare to risk, we refuse to worry, because we trust God to guide and take care of us.

How do we acquire this faith in the first place? In Romans 10 Paul talks about how people come to faith, through which they are saved. This is the faith which 'calls on the name of the Lord' (Romans 10:13). He asks how anyone can call on someone in whom they do not believe, or believe in someone of whom they have not heard. 'So,' he says, 'faith comes by what is heard' (or nowadays we might add, by what is read) of Christ. Paul talks of more than mere believing, though: he speaks of obeying the good news and bemoans the faithlessness of the Israelites, who were a 'disobedient and contrary people'. Trusting enough to obey is an integral part of faith. It is not enough to have feelings of trust if this does not result in obedient choices, decisions and actions.

This is seen, above all, in the famous chapter on faith, Hebrews 11, where the writer gives a long list of people who showed their faith by what they *did* in response to God. By faith, Noah, warned by God, built an ark; by faith, Abraham obeyed, when he was called and set out, not knowing where he was going; by faith, Moses chose to share ill-treatment with the people of God, rather than to enjoy the fleeting pleasures of sin; by faith, the people crossed the Red Sea; by faith ...; by faith ...; by faith ...; so the catalogue goes on. Faith produces response and action.

Thus, Christian faith has these two main aspects, belief and active trust. It comes by hearing about Jesus Christ and responding to him. How, then, does it increase and grow? Most living things grow by food and exercise. So what food and exercise does faith need?

The food of faith is surely truth, especially truth about God. All truth is good food – not just true facts, but also real encounter with God. Truth includes knowledge and understanding of the universe and all creation, science, the history of our planet and people and especially, God's revelation of himself through the history of the Jews and the life and work of Jesus Christ. These things help the believing side of our faith to grow, as we come to realize more of the infinite greatness and goodness of God, and his active love towards us. This enlarges our realization of how trustworthy he is. We are thus encouraged to entrust ourselves more fully to him and to his care.

Feeding our faith

The exercise of faith is to put such inner attitudes or feelings into action. This involves our conscious choice: we exercise our will to respond and to obey. We choose to let our decisions and actions change in the light of what we believe to be true about God and what he is asking of us. We step out in faith, much as Abraham did.

So how can we feed our faith with truth
about God? Do we need constant supplies of
new truth? God is an unfathomable mystery
and the source of 'boundless riches'
(Ephesians 3:8). There will always be plenty
more to discover and learn about him. Yet
much of what we find turns out to be not a
new truth, but a restatement, or rediscovery, of
truth we already know about God, that 'he
lives and loves and saves', as the hymn puts it.
Feeding our faith is usually a question of
reminding ourselves of old truths, although it
may be that fresh words and insights bring
those truths alive for us in new ways. I am
amazed how often my faith is boosted by a
simple restatement of the fact that God loves
us with a passionate love that shows itself in
action.

The Scriptures are the most obvious way of
reminding ourselves about what God is and
does. They are the word of God, his revelation
of himself and his saving acts, designed to
bring us to know God and build a relationship
with him.

Feeding our faith from the Scriptures will
involve our minds, as we study the Bible, trying to understand what it shows about God
and his ways of working, and how this applies
to us today. For example, we read that God is
love – but what kind of love? A love that plans
for our well-being (e.g. Jeremiah 29:11), not

necessarily by removing difficulties, but by promising to be alongside us and bring us safely through them (e.g. Isaiah 43:1-2; Psalm 23:4).

Feeding our faith from the Scriptures will also involve our feelings and our wills, as we seek to meet God in the Bible. We can enter the stories in our imagination, by stepping into them, or we can read and re-read passages as we would a love-letter, savouring and relishing them, and letting God speak to our hearts through them.

Our corporate worship – whether liturgical or not – also feeds our faith. Through Scripture readings, prayers, creed, Psalms and hymns, as well as the sermon, we are reminded of truths about God and helped to appreciate and apply them. We also see and experience the reality of God as we participate in worship together, especially in the sacraments of Baptism and Holy Communion. This is a vital part of the feeding of faith.

Faith is fed, too, by hearing about what God has done and is doing for all sorts of people. The Bible itself contains many such accounts, but we can find more in the stories of Christians down the years: lives of the saints and biographies, as well as books about more recent Christians. Personal testimony, whether given in public or merely in private conversation, can nourish our faith. We do well to listen to wise and mature Christians telling us what they have learnt from God over the years. In fact, any way in which another's heart tells our heart of its experience of God can help us.

We may be tempted to think that wonderful things happened a long time ago because things were different then, and that God is not doing such great things in people's lives today, especially in our own lives. Yet he is present and involved in all his creation. We *do* have experience of God. We may feel that our own experience of God is not very great – but never mind. It is ours and, even if it is not world-shattering or exciting to recount to others, it is the reality of what has happened to us. It is part of the truth about God. It reminds us of what we know of his love, his character and his individual treatment of us. We do well, therefore, to notice it, and keep remembering it with gratitude.

We do not need to be afraid or ashamed of our honest doubts and struggles of faith. They can drive us to a more earnest search for God and truth, from which our faith may well emerge stronger than before.

Those of us who have questions or doubts of an intellectual kind, or talk deeply with others who do, may need to feed our faith in this area too. It is not that intellectual or rational arguments can prove Christian belief, but they can support it and harmonize with it.

When we have intellectual doubts or questions, it can be very important to find some intellectually satisfying answers – even if only to see why we cannot expect to find a full answer – and not to be told simply that we should not be asking such questions (though such questions *may* at times be an excuse for not facing the demands or challenge of Christ). I have found C.S. Lewis's writings extremely helpful here. Once, when I was going through a difficult time, I questioned whether God really does anything to make a difference in the here-and-now in answer to our prayers. I tried hard to pray and to trust God to bring me through it, but this wasn't easy, especially when a little voice in my head began to say, 'Suppose there isn't really a God, after all? Suppose your Christian faith is just a game you've been playing?' I struggled on, trying to assert my faith as much as I could, until I realized that I was doing something rather foolish: I was trying to exercise my faith without feeding it.

I sensed that the food my faith needed at that stage was some of the writings of C.S. Lewis. I began to re-read *Mere Christianity* and *Miracles* and found them to be just what I needed: they wrestled with the questions I was asking, and provided some answers.

There are other writers whom I find helpful in other areas of Christian life. It is helpful if you know of authors with whom you 'click', and it's good to have books available, to which you are likely to return again and again.

We don't always know what particular kind of food our faith needs at any given time. That is one reason why regular church-going, Bible reading, fellowship and prayer are important, to provide a regular, varied and balanced diet for our faith.

Exercising our faith

What about exercising our faith? The first thing to remember is that we are trying to exercise the faith we actually have, not the faith we wish we had. Pretending is no use: it is only by putting to work whatever faith we have, whether great or small, strong or weak, that we will strengthen it.

We can think of exercising our faith as being like crossing a river on stepping-stones. We do not step first on to the stones in deep water, but on to the nearest stones, those in shallower water. Eventually it may feel like walking on water, but we do not start with what seems impossible and unbelievably risky. We start with what is possible for us, within our reach.

There is a saying about prayer: 'Pray as you can, not as you can't.' The same could be said of faith: 'Trust as you can, not as you can't.'

We must start from where we are now, our current situation, with the opportunities and challenges it presents to our faith, and with the degree of trust we actually have. We cannot, after all, be anywhere else – and if we don't begin now, when will we begin, and will it be any easier then?

A good starting-point for exercising faith is our prayers, especially our praise of God. In Romans 4:20, Paul says of Abraham, 'he grew strong in his faith as he gave glory to God'. Praising God is an affirmation of faith, an assertion of the goodness and greatness of God. Abraham's praise declared that he was trusting God's promise to do something that was incredibly unlikely, namely to give him and Sarah a son when they were about 100 years old. His praise was an exercise of faith, and one of the results was that his faith grew stronger. Moreover, God kept his promise and Isaac was born – which must also have boosted Abraham's faith somewhat!

We may not have a specific personal promise as Abraham had, but we do have the Bible, showing us God's nature and his promises to be with us, to care for us always and to bring us safely through this life to heaven. To praise God is to assert that we believe this, and that we trust him to be and do what he has promised. This exercises our faith, because we have

no advance proof that he will deliver the
goods.

Praise is even more of an exercise of faith
when circumstances are difficult, or we can see
little sign of God fulfilling his promises. It
requires great effort to choose to praise God
when we don't feel like it. Yet praise is the
affirmation that God is good, that he is ultimately in control and that we trust him to
bring something good out of every situation,
as he has promised (Romans 8:28). We trust
him, even though we cannot yet see how he is
working for our good.

Thanking God for what he has done – in our
own lives or other people's – builds faith in
much the same way as praise does, as it means
that we keep looking at what we have already
seen of God's good activity. It reminds us of
what we know through experience of the
goodness of God.

In intercession, too, we can exercise our
faith. The very act of taking the time and
trouble to bring to God our concerns for
other people, indicates that we think there is
some chance that God is there and listening,
and that he might do something in response.
The greater our trust in God, the more confi-
dently we are able to pray – but whatever the
quality of our faith, it will grow as we inter-
cede, especially when we see answers to our
prayers. Seeking not to fret, but to wait

patiently for the answers can be an exercise of faith too.

Obedience

Obeying God is exercising faith, because it is acting on the belief that what God tells us to do is good and worthwhile. Obedience to what we believe God wants can involve simple activities, such as praying, or going to church, or being nice to people, even when we do not feel like it. But obedience also extends to such issues as our use of money – the proportion we give to God's work and the way we use the rest. We can express obedience, too, in being willing to stand up for what we believe to be right, even at the risk of ridicule or persecution.

When we suffer, whether physically, mentally, or in any other way, we may be tempted to doubt God's loving care, or his ability to help us in our pain. We can exercise faith during those times by continuing to cry to him for help, trusting him as best we can, holding on to him, even if only by our fingernails.

During dry or desert times, when we have no sense of God's presence or love, we exercise our faith by continuing to pray, worship and obey God, even though we do not seem to get anything out of it. We do these things because we think that, although we are not aware of him, God may yet be there and is worth serving for his own sake, not just for the sake of our own feel-good factor.

We cannot arrange these different ways of exercising faith in any order of strength, or difficulty, because what is hard for one person may be easy for another, and vice versa. One person may find it easy to trust God over money and yet find it hard to trust him with their health. Someone who is willing to endure ridicule for their faith, or persecution for standing up for a principle, may find it hard to trust in God's unconditional love and acceptance of them as a person.

Sometimes, when we exercise our faith in any of these ways, God acts marvellously, giving great answers to our prayers, and our faith grows almost visibly. At other times, we do not get the answers for which we were hoping, but in the process of exercising our trust we discover more of God and his love through what he provides to sustain us, and we come to recognize more of the good qualities that he is producing within us. This, too, can strengthen our faith.

The feeding and exercising of faith can be finely interwoven. We feed our faith, increasing our understanding, or belief. As a result, we decide to act differently, perhaps taking what feel like bigger risks, thus exercising our faith. If we find that God blesses, maybe through a good outcome of our actions, through a greater inner peace, or through discovering more of God and his love, we have more evidence that God is trustworthy and good.

We should not be discouraged if our faith is small and weak. Jesus said that faith the size of a mustard seed could accomplish great things (if encouraged to grow!). And it has the potential to grow into something much bigger.

A prayer

Lord, sometimes faith seems such a complex and difficult thing. We would like to find ways of making it grow instantly, yet much of its growth is slow and hidden from our view. Help us to go on nourishing and using whatever faith we have. Work in us by your Spirit, so that when testing times come, we are able to hold on to you. Thank you that you will hold on to us, and can use even such experiences to strengthen our faith; through Jesus Christ, our Lord. Amen.

5

Does God use me more than I realize?

Our lives touch the lives of other people all the time. They may criss-cross a particular person's life on many occasions, and God can use those occasions in ways whose significance we hardly realize, weaving them together to create something good and beautiful. Experience has taught me that we shouldn't give up praying for our friends, even when our lives are moving apart from theirs.

Liz (not her real name) is a friend of mine from student days. While we were at university, I longed for her to become a Christian. I prayed for Liz, and sometimes talked with her about God, Jesus and the Christian faith – but she wasn't very interested. I also tried to persuade her to come to church, or to meetings where she would hear the Christian message presented better than in our conversations, but

she never came. When we left university, I
thought that I had failed – Liz had not become
a Christian, and now she probably never
would. After all (I thought in my arrogance),
when would she have such opportunities
again?

After leaving university, we kept in touch at
Christmas and occasionally at other times. I
did continue to pray for her sometimes, but
without much expectation that anything
would happen.

When Liz married, she and her husband
John were clear that they were definitely not
Christians. When their two children Sally and
David were born, they took definite and posi-
tive decisions each time not to have them
baptized.

One day, as Liz walked, with the two
children in a pushchair, into the Scottish vil-
lage where they lived, she suddenly felt as
if she just *had* to go into the church. The priest
was inside and welcomed her. She sat quietly
in the church for a while, then left. That
was all.

Soon after this, Liz, John and the children
were walking in some woods and came to a
full, fast-flowing stream. There was a log laid
across and John, Liz and David, aged about
two, climbed on to it and stood watching the
water flowing past. Suddenly the log tipped
and they were all plunged into the icy water.

David, face down began to float away down-
stream. Liz managed to pull him out and
flung him on to the bank, breaking his leg in
the process as they later discovered! John was
yelling, most uncharacteristically – he was
pinned down by the log with his face only just
clear of the water. Liz was afraid the log might
descend further, crushing him, or pushing him
under. She tried to pull it off, but it was too
heavy. Mercifully, some passers-by eventually
heard their calls for help and came and rescued them.

These two events – the urge to go into
church and the accident, which could so easily
have ended in tragedy – turned Liz's thoughts
to God. Having known from student days that
I was a Christian, she wrote to me for help.
She says now that if she couldn't have contact-
ed me, she wouldn't have known where to
turn.

Meanwhile, I was married, with three children under the age of four. Life seemed to be
all food and bottoms, and I was feeling like a
bit of a cabbage, and not much use to God.
(With hindsight, I think I undervalued my caring for the family as work for God.) My husband suggested that, if I could not get out and
do things for God, perhaps I should ask God to
send people to me. I took his advice and
prayed that God would send me opportunities
to serve him.

Within a week, Liz's letter arrived: 'Dear Molly, you may wonder why I am writing to you out of the blue like this, but I want to know more about Jesus...' – and asking me to help her to do that. I was delighted to do so. After that, we kept in closer touch for a while, and to my great joy, Liz became a committed Christian, growing in her faith, and getting involved in a healing and counselling ministry.

I am not a good letter-writer, and lapsed again into writing only once or twice a year, although I did pray a little more often. Several years later, Liz suddenly kept coming to my mind and I began to pray in a much more concentrated way for her. I also wrote to tell her that this was happening and to re-establish closer contact. It transpired that she had just given up teaching, and was feeling a bit depressed and useless. My letter was like a touch of God's love to encourage her. Since then, we have managed to maintain better contact. Liz is continuing her counselling while also studying theology, now that her children are grown up.

All this leaves me wondering at the ways of God, weaving together the tapestry of our lives – not just Liz's and mine, but everyone's, working for good in every way possible. It reminds me of the story of Philip and the Ethiopian eunuch in Acts 8. History does not describe the eunuch's journey, but God led Philip, first by an angel and then by the Spirit, to get him and the eunuch to the same place at the same time. There they had an encounter that was life-changing for the eunuch, perhaps for Philip too.

Since God is always present and involved with his creation, I don't think it's possible to draw a sharp distinction between his 'natural' and 'supernatural' ways of working. Thus I can't say exactly how responsible God was for the fact that Liz and I were at the same college, reading the same subject at the same time. Nor do I know if it was his nudge that prompted her to write to me about finding Jesus, or he who laid her on my mind when she was depressed, years later. Yet I do know that he used those times to help and encourage us both. When we follow a hunch in reaching out to someone, it may be a nudge from God as part of his good purposes: the right touch at the right time in that person's life.

I know too that I thought my student attempts to tell Liz about Jesus were a dismal failure. Yet they played a part in her journey towards Christ, all the same. We may think we have been ineffective – but who can tell what God may yet make out of our feeble efforts, when something is remembered years later? God doesn't stop working, even when we are not on the spot to help him! The interweaving of our lives with other people's may not be wasted, the effects not finished when we move apart.

A prayer

Father, we marvel at how you can work for good in all our lives at once and still manage to take everything into account. Thank you that you can use us more than we realise, in spite of our weakness and lack of faith. Keep us alert to the opportunities you give us. Teach us to recognise and trust the nudges of your Spirit, and help us to pray for those you lay on our hearts and not to give up hope; in Jesus' name. Amen.

6

Will God grow tired of forgiving me?

Have you ever been on the merry-go-round (actually more of a miserable-go-round!) of wondering whether or not you have really repented, when you keep coming to confess the same old sins over and over again? It easily leads to doubting that you have been forgiven and it can make you feel such a hypocrite: 'I don't deserve to be forgiven if I'm not truly sorry.'

In our family we had a saying, '"Sorry" means I won't do it again.' We didn't mean, 'Your "sorry" is only good enough if you never repeat the mistake.' The thinking behind it was to help the children not just to use 'sorry' as a word to get them out of trouble, but to say it with an attitude of regret and the intention to change behaviour. In the same way, saying sorry to God should carry a similar sense of regret and intention to change.

The Greek word for repentance, *metanoia*, means a change of mind, a turning back from our own way towards God's way. The link between confession, saying sorry, and the intention to change is clear throughout the Bible.

When people tried merely offering sacrifices and then going off to sin again, the Old Testament prophets thundered against them. For example: 'Trample my courts no more; bringing offerings is futile ... Cease to do evil, learn to do good' (Isaiah 1:12, 17). Outward signs of repentance, like putting on sackcloth and ashes, or tearing one's clothes, were no use if there was no change of heart. As Joel says, 'Rend your hearts and not your clothing' (Joel 2:13). In the New Testament, John the Baptist told the Pharisees to 'Bear fruits worthy of repentance' (Luke 3:8). Jesus' first call, also, is, 'repent', and then 'Follow me' (Mark 1:15, 17).

So far so good. But changing, or being changed, is not as easy as all that. We may manage to alter our behaviour quite easily in some respects, but other habits are very deep-rooted in our background and our personality, with all its fears and weaknesses. Repentance means turning from what is wrong to what is right, but though we may turn and start on the right path, we cannot always manage to keep going in that direction.

This is where we climb on to the merry-go-round. I have done it many times myself. The thought-process goes something like this: 'If I repent of a sin, I turn away from it. If I turn away from it completely, I will never choose to commit that sin again, though I may have the occasional slip-up. Therefore, if I keep repeating the sin, there must be something in me that wants to do it. Thus I cannot have turned away from it fully. I have not really repented, I should not have the cheek to ask God for forgiveness. I doubt whether God *can* forgive me for the same sin over and over again, not because his grace and mercy are insufficient, but because I am not truly sorry.'

My own way of handling this problem in the past was to refrain from confessing the sins, for fear of being a hypocrite. It was honest – but not a very good solution, because it left me rather stuck: wanting to change, yet unable to do so. What could I do?

Eventually I realized that I was making two assumptions. One was that I could only confess something when I had fully repented of it – but this isn't true. I can acknowledge that I have done wrong and that I want and need forgiveness and help, even though I know I don't have the strength to do what is right.

The second assumption was that repentance implied a promise never to do it again; that I could only really have repented when *everything* in me was determined always to choose what was right. Yet when something has its roots deep in our personality, our background and our habits, we are most unlikely to be able to change it quickly. Instead, we need to be made more whole, which is an ongoing process – and we need time to build new habits and patterns of behaviour. Of course, God might do this for us instantly, but we cannot demand that he does so. We must have patterns of confessing and repenting which help us to carry on when God is working more slowly.

How does this help us get off the merry-go-round? It helps us to see that we can never guarantee not to commit a particular sin again. For one thing, the better we know ourselves, the more we realize how weak we are, how vulnerable to cracking under pressure. God doesn't expect us to succeed on our own. The Psalmist says, 'He knows how we were made; he remembers that we are dust' (Psalm 103:14); and Jesus says, 'Apart from me you can do nothing' (John 15:5).

True repentance does not imply a guarantee never to do it again. Rather, in repenting, we set ourselves to face God's way, expressing our intentions for the future, saying, 'This is the way I choose and now intend to go.' We cannot make our future choices now, only our present ones. We need not, therefore, feel burdened by guilt over the fact that we are unable to promise never to do it again. This realistic and humble view of ourselves may take us down a peg or two, but it is at the same time very liberating. It enables us to release a load we cannot bear.

It may also help us to realize that any worry over whether we have really repented is likely to concern our besetting sins – that is, our areas of inner sinfulness (pride, fear, self-centredness, etc.) which give rise to particular sinful acts, words or thoughts. God does want to heal us and deal with our inner problems, but at the right time, when he sees that we are ready for it and able to cope with it. Our continual coming to ask for forgiveness may be an important part of the healing and growing process. It is part of our becoming more ready and willing for change, as our repeated failure increases our sense of helplessness and dependence on God.

Above all, we must confront what may be the greatest flaw of all in the thinking that gets us on to the merry-go-round: we forget the work of the Holy Spirit. Yet it is the Spirit who convicts us of sin and urges us towards God for forgiveness and help. It is the Spirit who prompts our repentance, our desire to go God's way rather than our own. And it is the Spirit who strengthens us to resist evil and choose what is right. If we were left to our own devices and our own strength, our prospects would be hopeless, but we belong to Christ, we have God's Spirit living and working in us. We are not promised instant perfection, but we are promised that God's work of making us whole and Christ-like will one day be complete. 'The one who has begun a good work among you will bring it to completion by the day of Jesus Christ' (Philippians 1:6).

Many of us begin our Christian life knowing that we need merely to receive God's forgiveness in childlike trust, contributing nothing of our own. We just hold out empty hands to receive what God gives us; forgiveness, love and the life of his Spirit within us. We are liable, however, to keep slipping away from this dependence on God and his grace into thinking we can do the right thing on our own.

So, have we really repented? The measure of this doesn't lie in our ability to promise never to do it again in the future. It probably isn't the best question to be asking anyway, since it is concerned with the past. A better question is, 'Am I really repenting now?' I am really repenting now if I am choosing, as genuinely as I know how (no more is required), to ask

God's forgiveness for my sins and offering him my resolve (imperfect though it may be), to go his way in future. At the same time, I need to ask for the Spirit to strengthen me to carry out my resolve.

When we fail, it is not because our repentance is false, but because God's work of making us whole is not yet finished. We can go on, trusting in the mercy and love of our God, who does not despise a 'broken and contrite heart' (Psalm 51:17). We can keep on coming to the throne of grace, 'so that we may receive mercy and find grace to help in time of need' (Hebrews 4:16).

A prayer

Loving Father, forgive us our foolish ways. Forgive us the arrogance that leads us to try and sort ourselves out before coming to you. Thank you for your never-failing love, always reaching out to us, ready to pick us up and stand us on our feet again. Thank you for the gift of your Spirit to help us; through Jesus Christ, our Lord. Amen.

7

Are there places where God will not meet me?

When we worry about putting ourselves beyond God's reach, we may be thinking or feeling things like, 'I shouldn't be in this situation at all', or 'I can't expect God to come to me, I must get myself to him', or 'My problem or situation is too difficult for him'.

In some ways, it may seem that the answer to the question posed in the title of this chapter is obvious, God can meet us anywhere, because he can be everywhere all the time. But the limitation is ours: since each of us can only ever be in one place at a time, where we are is the only place where we are available. It is only from there that God can take us forward. This sense of place includes not only our external circumstances, but also what is within us, our character and attitudes, our thoughts and feelings, hopes and fears. The question we really want answered may be to do with whether God is able and willing to come and help us in situations that we regard as either hopelessly difficult, or our own fault. Yet the real God will deal with the real us, in our actual circumstances in the real world. It is useless to pretend. God knows where we are and will come to meet us there.

When we doubt God's ability to meet us wherever we happen to be, we are, by implication, believing that we have to dig ourselves out of our own holes. Yet the whole point of Jesus' coming into the world to live and die for us is that we are unable to get out of the holes by ourselves. We cannot make ourselves righteous, or whole. We cannot by ourselves put right the evils of the world and ensure that justice prevails. This can sound like bad news – but the good news is that God is fully aware of our weakness and is more than ready to come to us on this basis. The Bible's word for this is 'grace'.

God's coming to rescue people in predicaments from which they cannot rescue themselves is the story of the Bible. One of the foundation stories of the Jewish-Christian tradition tells of how God rescued the Israelites from slavery in Egypt. I love the passage when God appears to Moses in the burning bush, declaring, 'I have heard their cry … I know their sufferings, and I have come down to deliver them' (Exodus 3:7-8). The sequence of those three verbs is so wonderfully understanding and hope-giving: 'I have heard ... I know ... and I have come'.

The greatest rescue-job of all – rescuing the world from the clutches of evil and death – was done by Jesus. As Paul writes, 'God proves his love for us in that while we still were sinners Christ died for us' (Romans 5:8). And the writer to the Hebrews urges us to 'approach the throne of grace with boldness, so that we may receive mercy and find grace to help in time of need' (Hebrews 4:16). This promise holds true regardless of whether our predicament is our own fault or not.

Slipping into discouragement or self-deception – thinking 'It all depends on me and I can't do it' – can happen quite subtly at times. When coming to pray, I can easily slip into thinking that God's help starts only when I have got myself in step with him, praying 'according to his will', and aligning my will with his. Yet I actually need help in order to do this, so I must call upon him from the very start. In acknowledging that I don't know how to pray, I am actually being more real with God than if I tried to convince myself that I had everything worked out. Admitting my helplessness throws me back on God's grace again. And that is a good place to be.

We may also get discouraged if we know
that there is something we need to put right in
our life, but it seems almost impossible to do.
We may need to forgive someone, for example.
We can't come to God, we think, to ask him
what to do, because we *know* what has to be
done. Our difficulty lies in doing it. We think
we can only meet God and move forward spiritually after we have done the forgiving, or
putting right. Yet it may well be that our spiritual progress lies in the very discovery that we
cannot put things right on our own. 'The spirit indeed is willing, but the flesh is weak'
(Matthew 26:41). We need to admit our weakness to God, telling him that we want to
choose what is right and asking for the
strength to do it. God will meet us where we
are, and take us on from there. In Jesus' story
of the tax collector and the Pharisee (Luke
18:9-14), it is the tax collector, who admits his
failure and asks God for mercy, who moves
forward spiritually, not the Pharisee who talks
to God about his successes.

God's invitation is always to call on him
immediately, as soon as possible – as Isaiah
urges, 'Seek the Lord while he may be found,
call upon him while he is near' (Isaiah 55:6).

He may, of course, come unbidden. There
are many examples of that not only in the
Bible, but throughout Christian history. He
came to Abraham, who was sitting at the

entrance to his tent, and promised him a
son. He came to Moses, and later to David,
while they were looking after sheep, to call
them to great tasks. He came to a very
depressed and discouraged Elijah in the
desert, to set him on his feet again. And when
Jonah was in a fish's belly, having really let
God down, God came to rescue him and give
him another chance. Jesus came and called
several of his disciples as they were fishing or
tax-collecting. After his resurrection, he came
to Mary Magdalene grieving in a garden, to
the disciples in an upper room and on the
beach and to two others as they walked home.
God came to each of these people, just where
they were, whatever they were doing and
however they were feeling.

Sometimes our sense of 'stuckness', or of
God being far away, can be a consequence of
wilful, or persistent sin and disobedience. If
this is the case, repentance 'unsticks' things
and enables God to draw near and help us.
Always he longs to welcome those who turn
back to him and go his way: 'Let them return
to the Lord, that he may have mercy on them,
and to our God, for he will abundantly par-
don' (Isaiah 55:7). Jesus' picture of the father
running out to welcome his prodigal son and
celebrating his home-coming illustrates God's
eagerness to respond to any of his children
who reach out to him for forgiveness and help.

God meets us wherever we are, but because he wants the very best for us, he leads us on to a better place. That isn't always a comfortable or easy journey. It may well be challenging and humbling, but if we are going with God it is always worthwhile, because his plans for us are always positive, always good. To Jewish exiles in danger of discouragement, God says, through Jeremiah, 'I know the plans I have for you, ... plans for your welfare and not for harm, to give you a future with hope' (Jeremiah 29:11). He is the same God, who would say the same to his people today.

He is able to reach us, wherever we are. For one thing, he always knows where we are. Psalm 139 speaks of many places where we might think we can hide from God, as high, low, or far away as we can imagine – but God is in every place. I have a friend who was found by God in prison. Nor are we hidden from him in the dark, for darkness is as light to him (verse 12). Even the penitent thief on the cross next to Jesus was not beyond God's reach in the last desperate hours of his life.

God always knows how to lead us forward. It does not matter whether we ourselves can see how to proceed or not. We may wish things undone, so that we could go back to some previous, 'better' situation and start again, but that is not only impossible, it is unnecessary. God can use whatever has happened, and work through it for our good, however unlikely that may seem. That is what Paul means in Romans 8:28 where he says, 'We know that *all* things work together for good for those who love God' (the italics are mine).

So there is no utterly hopeless position to be in, no situation where God cannot reach us, no problem too hard for him. If we have in us only a spark of wanting, of reaching out to God, there is hope.

A prayer

Almighty God, thank you that you can reach us no matter how dark our situation, that you can hear us no matter how feeble our cry. Thank you for your goodwill towards us, your desire to meet us anywhere and take us on from there. You are slow to anger and of great kindness; help us to trust your love, and your commitment to us; keep us from discouragement and despair; for Jesus' sake. Amen.

8

How can I let Christ transform my regrets?

Many of us struggle to come to terms with events and circumstances in our past that we wish we could change. It is all too easy to hanker after what might have been, if only circumstances had been different.

I recall hearing a story once about a man who refused what he believed was God's call to be a missionary. He was ordained instead, but for years felt that, although his ministry had some value, it was very much a second-best compared with what God had really wanted for him. This went on even though he had greatly regretted his earlier disobedience many years before, had confessed it to God and knew that he was forgiven. When his children grew up and left home, he told God once again that he was sorry for having failed to respond before, but that he was now willing to go to the mission field. Interestingly, the man felt that God no longer wished him to be a missionary. That had been a call in the past, but his calling now – as it had been for a long time – was to the ordained ministry in England.

The point of the story is that God doesn't start with a fixed plan for us, and, when we fail to follow it, go to his second-best plan, and then to the third best, and so on. If that were the case, each of us, as our life passed by, would become more and more of a disappointment to God. The message is, rather, that at every moment, however much or little we have conformed our lives to his will so far, God has a call to us, something he really wants us to do *now*. We need to respond to the call of the present moment, and not remain in a state of perpetual regret over failing to respond to the calls of earlier times

It is not only our *own* bad choices that can lead us to hanker after what might have been. The course of our lives is also greatly affected by what other people have done or not done, and by events for which no one is particularly responsible. We may at times say, or think, 'If only ...' about any of these things: 'If only he (or she, or they) had not ...', 'If only I had ...', 'If only things had been different', and 'If only I could have my time over again.' If only ..., if only ..., if only ... .

Some years ago, I was preparing a sermon on John 21, where, after the resurrection, Jesus asks Peter three times if he loves him, and three times says, 'Feed my sheep.' This three-fold pattern matches Peter's earlier three-fold denial of Jesus. I thought of some 'If onlys' that Peter may have been struggling with – such as, 'If only I hadn't denied him', or, 'If only I hadn't gone to the high priest's house.' Suddenly the phrase came to me, 'God is not a God of "'If only".' This phrase struck me quite powerfully, and when I used it in the sermon, it seemed to strike other people too. I realized what a common thing it is for people to think in terms of 'If only', and therefore, how important it is to learn that we need not hanker after what might have been, because God is not a God of 'If only'.

There are several disadvantages to living with an 'If only', a perpetual regret. The very pain of habitually thinking and feeling that what you are and do is not really what God wanted, nor as good as it might have been, is a constant drain on our energy and our joy. It may also weaken our faith: if deep down we do not trust that God has *fully* dealt with our past, we are less likely to trust him fully in the present or future. The sense of not being in God's ideal place for us may also mean that we are not as committed as we should be to our present situation, since we are not sure that we should be there.

Other problems can arise, if knowingly or unknowingly we are harbouring resentments about past events, whether against another person, against ourselves, or against God. Resentment of any kind hinders spiritual growth, because it is so much the opposite of mercy, grace and forgiveness – the characteristics of God. Spiritual growth is becoming *more* like God, not less like him – and so hanging on to resentment is the same as refusing to become more like God. Jesus taught that having our own sins forgiven is very closely linked to our ability to forgive those who wrong us. It is not always easy to forgive, especially when we feel our lives have been significantly damaged by what has happened, or when we have hung on to our resentment for a long time – but God will help us if we want him to.

It would be wonderful not to live with any 'If onlys'. The whole Bible tells us again and again that God loves to welcome and forgive people, and give them a new, clean start, without any carrying forward of 'If onlys', from the past – but can we believe that *we* could be free of them?

'If only they hadn't . . .'

We can be free of regrets about what other people have done to us.

The Old Testament story of Joseph demonstrates this well. Joseph was a favourite son, spoilt brat who so annoyed his older brothers that they almost killed him, but instead sold him to be a slave in Egypt. Through his position he saved many people from famine, both in Egypt and the surrounding countries, including his own brothers and their families. After their father's death, his brothers feared Joseph's revenge for the way they had mistreated him all those years before. But what Joseph says to them is remarkable in its insight: 'Do not be afraid!... Even though you intended to do harm to me, God intended it for good, in order to preserve a numerous people, as he is doing today' (Genesis 50:19-20). Joseph knew that God had brought good out of his brothers' sins, not only for Joseph himself, but also for his brothers and for thousands of other people. This was a cause not for regret or retaliation, but for thanksgiving.

A few years ago, I applied to do a course about an area of Christian ministry. It seemed to me that various aspects of my previous experience covered most of the first year of the course and I knew that others were exempted from it, so I asked to be exempted too. I requested this before the course started and again a few sessions into it, while there was still time to transfer. I was refused both times.

I felt I had not been really listened to or understood which I found very hard.

When praying, I had told God that I would accept the decision whatever it was and look for good to come out of it. So that was what I tried to do.

It turned out to be true that I had covered much of the work before. I was bored and frustrated and I often thought, 'If only they hadn't made me go through this.' However, having told God I would go along with the decision, I also looked for what was positive. This included more practice of accepting and making the best of other people's mistakes (as I saw it) and forgiving them; learning to turn my own frustration into something more positive; and finding better ways of coping with what felt like a rejection of myself and my spirituality.

At the end of the year, I decided to tell the leaders that I still felt that a mistake had been made and what I thought might be done to avoid similar mistakes in future. It would have been more usual for me to say nothing to them, while continuing to think 'If only…'. Taking responsibility for doing something about it by speaking out on my own behalf was, I think, a real sign of growth. It also led to another positive outcome, in that my criticism was accepted and an apology given. I was not looking for that, but it rewarded my courage in a way that was very affirming.

Looking back on the whole experience, I regard it as positive. I find I have no resentment and I am thankful that, although mistakes were made, through them, with God's help, I was able to grow into greater peace and maturity. My memories of that time do not include the words 'If only'.

'If only I hadn't . . .'

Some of our regrets about our own behaviour arise because of the ways in which we have hurt other people; some are because of the consequences in our own lives.

When I was 13 I was involved in a road accident and spent a week in hospital, in an adult ward. The lady in the next bed (whose name I forgot long ago, so I shall call her Mrs X) was very ill. She was cheerful, though, and kind to me. One night, towards the end of my stay, Mrs X was moved to a screened-off bed near the Sister's office, and some people came to be with her. In the morning she had gone. 'Moved to another ward,' said a nurse, but I did not believe her and she did not deny it when I asked her straight if Mrs X had died.

What upset me most wasn't the fact that Mrs X had died - of course I was sorry about it, but it was probably a welcome release from her suffering. No, what upset me most was the fact that I had not told her about Jesus. I assumed that she had no Christian faith, although I can't now remember what evidence I had for that opinion. My own faith was very immature at the time, and maybe nothing I could have said would have helped Mrs X in the slightest. Nevertheless, I often wished I had said something to her and thought that if only I had it might have made a difference to Mrs X, possibly even the difference between eternal life and death. I now have greater confidence in the loving justice and mercy of God; I am sure that he knew what Mrs X's response to Jesus was and would have been. Her eternal destiny did not depend only, or perhaps at all, on what might have been said to her at the time of her death, especially by me. My feelings of guilt may well have been unjustified, but the fact remains that I said nothing and regretted it.

Since then, I have come to see that the very experience of regret for this failure increased my desire to seize any opportunity God gives me to tell people about him. I have learned, too, that not only do I need to come to God for forgiveness, but I also have to put my failures and their consequences into God's hands and leave them there.

Another 'If only' began when, at the beginning of one school term, I made a decision which affected me for a long time: I was elected as form monitor and declined to accept it. Part of my reason was that I thought the form had elected me as a joke, because I had been in all sorts of mischief during the previous two years! The form denied any joke, but I found it hard to believe. The other part of my reason was that I was afraid of doing the job badly, because I was not sure of all that it involved. Almost as soon as I had made it, I regretted my decision as cowardly, but felt I couldn't do anything about it. Over the next few years, I was never elected monitor again, nor chosen as a school prefect, nor to hold some other positions I would have liked at school and university. I felt that if only I hadn't ducked out that first time, I would probably have developed greater confidence and leadership, and ultimately achieved more.

As it was, I came to believe that being 'not chosen' was the pattern of my life. This may or may not have been true – but it was what I believed about myself. The way out of this attitude came many years later, and consisted, among other things, in recognizing the good that came from the experience – even from the 'If-only-I-hadn't-spoilt-my-own-chances' way of thinking that arose out of it. The process of growth out of my 'If only' attitude was not free of pain; I had to face the hurt and damage I had caused myself, as well as the good God had brought about. The good, however, really *is* good: sympathy and understanding for those who blame themselves, together with the discovery, through my own healing, and through seeing others go through a similar process, that we do not need to stay stuck in that way of thinking.

In order to move forward with freedom, hope and a sense of purpose, we need to let go of the past in a way that really deals with the issues. We need to face the hurts, grieve for them where necessary, and let go of them, asking God to heal any residual emotional or other wounds. We need to forgive people and let go of any resentment. We need to recognize the good that God has brought out of our past, and we need to realize that God still calls us, to listen for that call and to respond to it. We need to come to the point where we can accept ourselves and our present situation, and commit ourselves to it in faith and hope.

'If only things had been different . . .'

We may think this way about all sorts of things, such as the looks and personality we were born with ('If only I were better looking', 'If only I were more sociable'); our position in the family, or our social environment ('If only I hadn't been the eldest', 'If only we'd been able to afford ...'); illnesses or misfortunes that affected us and those close to us ('If only we had been there', 'If only I had known'); or any circumstance in which we don't know whom to blame. Sometimes, deep down, we blame

God for these things, though we may not realize that that is what we are doing

It can be valuable to reflect on how good can grow from the most bitter experiences. A minister and his wife, who lost a child through a cot death, used their agonizing experience to help others in similar distress. They set up a scheme with local doctors, through which people were given time to talk and received sympathetic listening. This couple are now based at a cathedral which reaches out to 'unsuccessful' and damaged people as a very important aspect of its ministry. This work is so important that someone is only considered for a position on the staff if they have had some personal experience of pain or wounding. God has surely brought good for many out of one couple's awful experience of their child's death.

I can think also of two women whose lives of faith blossomed following the death of their husbands. In one case, the woman was drawn into the life of the church and came to personal faith, through the pastoral care and friendship she received from the church in her bereavement. In due course, she became a carer and friend to many others, doing babysitting, house-sitting and visiting elderly and bereaved people.

The other woman was already a committed Christian, very involved in the church, but through her loss and pain she discovered God's love for her in a much deeper way. She also discovered that she had gifts of compassion, counselling and healing prayer for others, which she has had the time and freedom to develop and use, not only in her local church, but also more widely.

An instinctive reaction to this is, 'If only these women's husbands could have had this blossoming of faith and ministry along with their wives.' I know that at least one of these wives has struggled with such thoughts. And yet, at the same time, I know that it was partly *because* of the loss of their husbands that the women themselves sought God and grew in their faith and sense of purpose.

So when we look at the good that God has brought about, do we say, 'That was why God allowed the men to die: it was worth all the suffering of bereavement, for the good that came out of it'? No, I don't think we can say that – we don't know the whole mind of God. The reasons why and when God allows things are complex and must take account of all factors of a situation, not merely the few aspects that *we* can see. What we can say is that God knows what he is doing, that his will is for everyone's greatest good and that we sometimes see some of the good that he can bring out of sad events.

If we blame God for what has happened, we can safely express our anger and other feelings to him. There is a long tradition of telling God what you think of him (see, for example, Psalms 13; 38; 77:1-10; 88). Eventually, however, we need to come to the point of 'forgiving' God by letting go of our resentment against him. We can do this more readily if we can see the good he has brought, and wants to bring, out of a situation. It is possible for us to come to a position of thankfulness, not for the pain itself, nor for any sin, but for the good that God has brought out of it. We cannot change the events of the past, but we can be changed in our perceptions and attitudes. I once heard a Jesuit priest say that the three worst experiences of his life were also the best.

I have found it helpful, when thinking about 'If onlys', to remember Jesus' crucifixion. He was put to death as a result of many people's sins: the sins of Judas, Caiaphas and Pilate, but also, in another sense, my sins and yours. Yet what Christian would say, 'If only Jesus had not died. If only he had lived to a ripe old age instead, how much better it would have been'? We don't say that, because we recognize that the good which God brought from the death of Jesus, namely salvation for the world, is so good that the desire to say 'Thank God' far outweighs the desire to say 'If only'. But that does not deny the sinfulness of many people's actions that led to the crucifixion.

In working to rid ourselves of regrets, it is good to have a wise, experienced Christian person alongside us to support us with love and prayer. This is especially important when the 'If only' is deep and goes back a long time, as we may find strong feelings arising that are hard to handle. In some cases we may need professional counselling. We also need to wait for God's own timing in these matters and not force things; he alone knows what we can cope with and when. He will bring things to the surface when we are ready to face them. When that moment comes, he can also provide someone to be alongside us who is able to help.

We shall minimize future 'If onlys' if we learn to be quick to forgive and if we look for how we can learn and grow in the situations we face each day, especially the hard ones. A good question to ask is always, 'What are you saying to me in this, Lord?' At any given moment, God's best plan is to meet us, call us, and take us on from where we are now, not from where we might have been, if only … We can learn to move forward in joy and hope.

A prayer

Thank you, Father, that you have been at work in all the events of our lives, even when we have not recognized you. Help us to see more and more how you have brought good out of our past. And help us not to hold things against any-one, so that we can work with you to bring the most good and the least harm, in all the experi-ences of life; through Jesus Christ our Lord. Amen.

9

What if God discovers how bad I really am?

If we are open to recognizing the truth about ourselves, we may be surprised, from time to time, by what we learn. The surprise may be a pleasant one, but, in my case at least, it is often not too nice. I discover myself to be more self-ish, proud, lazy, or whatever, than I had previously realized. I have heard people say that sometimes, when this happens to them, they are reluctant to approach God, because they think he no longer wants to relate to them, except in anger. A more helpful response is wanting to come to God all the more, because we have greater awareness of our need of him and his unconditional love.

Staying away from God when we discover more of our own sin and self-centredness is completely illogical. It is like saying that yesterday I thought God would accept me and be my friend, but today he will not want to be my friend any more because I am too self-centred, too unlovable. But today, what has actually changed? Only that *I* have found out that I am less nice than I thought I was. God has had no such surprise, and has made no new discovery. He knew yesterday all about the depths of self-centredness that I only discovered today, and he was prepared to relate to me then – so why not now? For that matter, he also knows already about anything I may discover tomorrow or the day after! In fact, he has known all that has been in me from the beginning, when he first sought me and called me into a relationship of love with him. And he is still committed to me and prepared to go on with me.

Not only this, but when God deals with any of us, it is never because we deserve his love or friendship. It is always on the basis of his perfect, unconditional love and grace, which he lavishes on us through Christ. Discovering how sinful we are doesn't change the basis of our relationship with God at all: that still rests entirely on his grace and mercy, brought to us through Jesus' death. The only difference is that we come a little nearer to appreciating how dependent we are on that grace.

There was a chorus we used to sing in Sunday school, of which I can remember only one (but surely the best) sentence: 'Jesus is the friend who knows the worst about you, and loves you just the same.' Is there anyone who doesn't need a friend like that? As we go through life, finding out more about ourselves and about God, we may have some unpleasant surprises about the depths of our own sin and selfishness – but God will have none. And we shall probably be surprised again by the depths of his love for us.

A prayer

Lord, you are my maker, you know me through and through, better than I know myself. Yet, knowing the worst, you are prepared to be my Saviour and my friend. Thank you for the utter security I have in depending on your grace. Help me never to forget or doubt it; for Jesus' sake. Amen.

10

How can I be open to whatever God wants for me?

The image of 'holding God's gifts on an open hand' is a vivid way of thinking about whether or not we trust God to know what he is doing with us, to give us all we need. It also concerns how we cope with loss.

It is a phrase which my husband, Graham, first used many years ago. It came to him in connection with a situation which he was finding rather difficult. He was in a new job, as part of a large staff, in which he found that all the aspects of ministry which he had previously regarded as his strengths were already being done by other people. After a while, all the tasks and ministries were put into the pool for redistribution, but when they were reallocated none was given to him! It felt as if all the ministries that God had given him earlier had been taken away. How was he to cope and react? As he prayed about it, the words, 'hold God's gifts on an open hand', were part of the answer God gave him.

To hold God's gifts on an open hand means giving God permission to take away things we value, if he sees fit, and to give us what *he* thinks we should have, for as long or short a time as he wants us to have them. It implies a trust in God to do the very best for us, both in what he gives and in what he takes away, and a willingness to accept his decisions.

This is relevant not only to our talents and ministries, but to all of God's gifts, including our money and possessions, the people who support and help us, our health and even our life. All is God's gift, so we are potentially considering anything and everything. We should, ideally, hold everything 'on an open hand'.

I am not saying that we should avoid commitment to the people and the responsibilities God gives us, nor am I suggesting that we should undervalue God's gifts, reject them, or be ungrateful for them. What I am saying is that we should not cling to people, possessions or status, that we should not regard them as 'ours' for ever, nor tell God to keep his hands off them.

Jesus told Mary Magdalene not to cling to him, when he met her after his resurrection. She was not to cling to the past, but must be ready to move on. This would involve loss, for she would not be able to see, or hear, or touch him, but there would also be gain, for he could now be close to her and to all his friends always. She would not lose Jesus, although it would seem like that at first. She had to give him his greater freedom and glory as the risen and later the ascended Lord.

In our relationships with other people, this 'holding on an open hand' also involves allowing them the freedom to move on. This can feel risky. The more committed we are to loving them, the more vulnerable we feel when we give them this freedom. They may choose to move on in a way, or at a time, that does not seem right to us. We fear we may get hurt. Our model in this vulnerability, however, is God himself, who commits himself utterly to us in love, while granting us the freedom to move away from him, if we choose. He, too, is vulnerable and gets hurt.

Where there has been love and commitment, the pain of loss and bereavement is healthy and good. We should not feel guilty about it. We need to grieve and mourn, but there comes a time when it is right to let go and move on to a new stage of valuing and remembering.

'Holding on an open hand' is important for our own growth and development. We become capable of new possibilities as our hands let go of old things in order to be able to take hold of new ones. When we lived in Coventry, my life was filled with many church activities: I was involved with outreach and drama groups, was a licensed reader on the staff of the church, and was on national and diocesan synods and committees. I was finding these responsibilities increasingly stressful. Then, when Graham was made Bishop of Willesden, we moved to London and I had to relinquish almost all of these responsibilities, which had its own stresses as I wondered what on earth I would do in our new situation. Yet it was a marvellous relief, as I was freed to grow in new directions, discovering and developing hitherto little used gifts and areas of ministry.

Being willing to let go is important as an expression of our faith in God. It declares that we trust him to know what is best for us and to give us gifts and opportunities for the well-being of others and of ourselves. If we try to retain his gifts, it is as if we doubt his wisdom, or his goodwill towards us, that we are afraid of what he might choose for us.

Perhaps more than anything else, this is a question of freedom. God allows us choices which may prevent him doing what he wants with us – so our choice to 'hold his gifts on an open hand' gives him greater freedom to do what is best, for us and for others.

It also means not being competitive in our ministry (whatever it may be) and in the

pastoral help we give. People are free to seek
help where they will, or no help at all. We have
to trust that God will guide them in their freedom to do what is best, or if they make bad
choices, that he will somehow bring good out
of it, and enable us to cope if we feel hurt.
Others with different gifts may be more able to
help at a particular time than we are. By being
willing to let go of some task, we may be pro-
viding an opportunity for someone else to
discover and develop a new gift or a new
ministry.

'Holding God's gifts on an open hand'
shows that we are sufficiently secure in
God's loving care for us not to need to cling to
other things for security. Choosing to 'hold
God's gifts on an open hand' increases our
freedom to launch out, to give ourselves to
God above all else. We are free to throw ourselves completely into anything he wants us to
do. We are also free to change direction, if that
is his call.

All this seems to open up tremendous possibilities. So why do we not always manage it?
Why are we not willing to relinquish this or
that ministry, this job in the church, or that bit
of status? Why are we less than fully generous
with our possessions, or so very cautious in
our management of money? Why do we cling
to our pastors? Why are we possessive of those
who look to us for support? Why, in other

words, do we find it hard to 'hold God's gifts on an open hand'?

Sometimes part of the answer is sheer self-ishness. We want to satisfy our own desires and preferences, and we want as much as pos-sible for ourselves. However, we are not total-ly self-focused. There is at least part of us that wants to be God-centred and, by his grace and his work in us, we become increasingly con-cerned for what pleases him. As this happens, we do generally find it easier to want God to work things out his way. Why, then, do we still find it difficult from time to time to give God a completely free hand with our lives?

We may feel that our sense of identity is closely bound up with what we see as our gifts and talents, and how we use them for God. The thought that we might give God permis-sion to take these things away is too frighten-ing, so we are unwilling to let go of our spheres of work, responsibility and ministry. We need to grasp fully the truth that our value and significance lie not in what we do, but in who we are. The most important and funda-mental aspect of our human identity is that we are made, loved and wanted by God, in spite of being sinners. Our *Christian* identity is that we are also forgiven sinners, accepted and united to God through Jesus Christ. That is where our value and significance lie – not in any abilities, roles or achievements.

Another reason why we cling to God's gifts may be that we fear that if God takes away what we have now, he will replace them with gifts we like less, or possibly no gifts at all. We must never forget that God is our loving father, who loves to give good things to his children (Matthew 7:11) and who gives gifts to all his people, for their part in his plans for the building up of his church and the well-being of all (1 Corinthians 12:4-11). His good gifts are not in short supply, and we should expect him to have some for us.

If we try to possess his gifts to boost our ego, or to find security in something other than God himself, he may choose to withdraw some of these gifts, in order to woo us back to himself and his priorities. If this happens, we need still to trust him and seek to learn what he has to teach us through the experience, painful though it may be.

The struggle to let God do what he wants in our lives often boils down to a lack of trust in him. We do not realize how good he is, or how worthy of our trust. We lack the confidence that he will provide us with whatever is necessary, both for our own needs and in order to serve him and other people. Yet in this, as in everything, we can ask him for grace to enable us to trust him more, knowing that he will gladly give it.

We need to remember God's infinite good-will towards us. He wants us all to be utterly secure in his love, knowing that he values us, and focusing on him, working with him for the good of all, whether our particular gifts and calling are to a large-scale work, or simply among our family and local community. To enable us to do this, he will provide us with whatever we need at any time. He asks us to 'hold his gifts on an open hand', so that we are free to move within his purposes and his plans for the good of all.

A prayer

Loving Father, thank you that you have your hand on our lives for good. Keep us trusting you to know what is best for us and even to strengthen us through times of loss. You are working in us for our good, and plan to use us to bring good to others. Help us not to spoil your work by clinging on to false securities, but to live in freedom, knowing that you will give us all we really need; through Jesus Christ, our Lord. Amen.

11

When God's way seems hard, how can I welcome it?

Shall we go God's way or our own? Choosing our own will rather than God's is what sin is all about. This is what has led to the alienation from God which is the basic problem of the whole human race. This is why we need forgiveness in order to be reconciled to God. This is why Jesus died. People come to Christ initially for a whole variety of reasons and with different needs uppermost in their minds – but somewhere there is usually an acknowledgement of not having lived as God wanted, and needing his forgiveness.

A fundamental part of being a Christian is that we turn from carelessly going our own way and seek to do what God wants. One of the earliest and simplest Christian creeds is 'Jesus is Lord', which implies that we give

Jesus the right to direct our lives and behaviour.

Yet many Christians know that, even after telling the Lord that we will do anything he asks of us, we later discover a situation in which we are not ready to say, 'Your will, not mine, no matter what.' It may be that we have not fully appreciated what it means to let God direct our lives, to allow him complete control of all our decisions. It may be that we still want the right to veto his suggestions in general. Or maybe there are a few areas of life in which we're too attached to particular people or things to allow God to have a free hand with us.

Where there is no desire, there is no temptation and no struggle. I have never had a struggle to resist the temptation to murder, because I have never wanted to murder anyone. I have only had to struggle with temptation when at least part of me has wanted to do something that God did not want me to do.

Sometimes our difficulty lies in trying to discern what we think God does want, which can be far from obvious. At other times we think we know what he wants, but it seems hard and we have difficulty in embracing it positively. God's will is always good, so we should expect that it will often lead to peace and enjoyment. We must beware of a negative and untrue view of God that leads us to think that what is hardest and least congenial is bound to be his will! In this chapter I have in mind times when we think we do know what he wants for us, but are finding the prospect hard.

It is encouraging to realize that Jesus did not always find it easy either. We tend to assume, because he chose to obey his Father at all times, and because he said he delighted in doing so, that he did not experience the kind of struggles that we do. But Jesus was fully human and 'in every respect ... tested [or tempted] as we are, yet without sin' (Hebrews 4:15). We should not be surprised, then, to find that he sometimes wanted, or partly wanted, things that were not God's will for him at that time.

At the very beginning of his public ministry, Jesus resisted the Devil's temptations in the wilderness, choosing God's way instead. But such choices are not made once for all. For Jesus, as for us, there was a continual choosing to do his Father's will. And on at least one occasion, this choice was a great struggle. In Gethsemane, as he faced the prospect of suffering and death, Jesus prayed, 'My Father, if it is possible, let this cup pass from me; yet not what I want but what you want' (Matthew 26:39). He truly shrank from the suffering and death to which his Father was calling him, and there was a real option open to him of avoiding it. He says, 'Do you think I cannot appeal to my Father, and he will at once send me more than twelve legions of angels?' (Matthew 26:53). I imagine that the twelve legions of angels were potentially available all through the Passion and that Jesus could at any stage have opted out of his suffering. In order to save the world as his Father had planned, however, he had to go on choosing what his Father wanted, rather than choosing to avoid his own pain, distress and alienation from God. We should not be surprised that we, too, have to go on and on choosing God's will rather than our own preference.

It has certainly been my experience that again and again I have to choose between what God wants and what I want. This choice is sometimes painful, because it is a question of self-denial, and in self-denial I am not only the one who is doing the denying, I am also the one who is being denied (which is almost always painful).

A useful reminder to motivate ourselves to choose God's will, is that he loves us more than we can appreciate, and what he sends is always the very best. It is true, though, that this 'best' is from a long-term point of view, not just what is most congenial in the short-term – and the aim is to produce faith, Christian character and the fruits of the Spirit. Yet, even at the moment of choosing what God

wants, we are likely to experience some benefits, such as peace and a sense of rightness in
our relationship with God.

Some time ago I discovered another unex-
pected benefit. It was at a time when other
people were making decisions that were
likely to cause me some difficulty. I thought
the decisions were mistaken, but was not
directly involved in the discussions. I was
aware that my opinion was biased, because I
knew that I would experience delay and probably some frustration too. I asked the Lord to
make my life easier, preferably by altering
some of the other people's decisions. I sensed
that his reply was that if their plans went
ahead things would indeed get harder, but
that he would bring great good out of it. I then
thought that he was asking me a question:
'Which will you choose: the hard way with
great good arising from it, or an easier way but
missing out on the good things I have in
mind?'

This was difficult. If I chose the easy way,
would he *really* change other people's plans to
make things significantly easier for me? I also
wondered whether the 'good things' he
offered were for me or for others, and if for
others, whether I would be unselfish enough
to choose the hard way for their sake alone?
And how hard would the hard way be? After
some hesitation and struggle, I said, 'If

the hard way is what you want, Lord, I'll choose that.'

I did experience delay. I had some health problems too, as it happened. It *was* hard, especially because for a while I had no sense of God's presence. Normally, I would have said, or thought, 'I wouldn't have chosen it to be this way.' This time, I couldn't say that. I *had* chosen it – not the details, but I had given God *carte blanche* to do what he wanted. Another time, I might have felt some anger, frustration or resentment against those whose arrangements and decisions had helped to make things hard. This time, I felt I had to bear some responsibility for the situation, so I wasn't angry or resentful, and only a little frustrated. The situation had been transformed because I had chosen to embrace whatever God wanted for me. It was as if we had chosen this path together and I was walking it with him, not reluctantly but positively, and expecting a good outcome.

The outcome was good, in many ways: the difficult circumstances weren't altered, but I learned useful lessons from them. Most of the health problems were eventually resolved, but not before I had come to surrender my life and health more fully into God's hands. My faith grew stronger, partly because God had brought me safely through the whole experience: I had learned to cope a little better with delay and frustration and was able to trust God more when things didn't work out the way I thought was right. My faith also grew partly because, in losing the sense of God's presence, I had spent time looking again at the foundations for faith, the reasons for believing in Christ and God. I was strengthened by my rediscovery yet again of the firm basis, in history, reason and in my personal experience, not only for the Christian faith but also for believing that God cares and knows what he is doing in my life.

Sometimes the choice we must make is about responding to situations in the way God wants – that is, in a Christ-like way – especially when people have hurt us. We always have a choice about our attitudes. Will we take our own share of responsibility or simply blame others? Will we resent or forgive? Will we nurse our hurt or let it go? We may know in our heart of hearts which is right – but which will we choose?

My experience at that time was that God seemed to give me the free choice of whether things were to work according to what he wanted, or according to what might be easier for me. This was only a particularly clear example of what is at stake every time we choose whether or not to co-operate with what appears to be God's will. When God's way seems hard, we have a range of options: 'No,

Lord, I am not willing for what you want. I'll resist it all the way'; or, 'I don't really want it, Lord, but I'll put up with it, if you insist'; or, 'I don't like the look of this, Lord, but I'll choose it because I trust your judgement'.

Whichever of these responses we make, events may turn out well, but there are particular benefits if we make the third, most positive response.

- We are freed from resentment, in that we cannot blame others when things are hard or painful for us, because we chose that hard path with God. We cannot blame God either, because he did not force us to choose his will.
- In our choice we have the opportunity to make a costly offering of love to God; we have denied ourselves for his sake, taken the risk of entrusting ourselves to him. This may not sound much like a benefit, but those who have experienced the joy of giving a desired and costly gift to someone they love deeply will know what I mean.
- There is a great sense of privilege in being invited by God to work in partnership with him, making choices together about the path to be followed.

A prayer

Loving Father, although we want to please you, we are also pulled towards pleasing ourselves. We admit that we are weak, so help us to trust more in your great love and goodwill towards us. Please give us the grace and strength to follow Jesus and to choose what you want for us, even when it seems hard; in Jesus' name. Amen.

12

How do I cope with my weaknesses?

Many of us struggle with our weaknesses, not least in those areas in which all Christians are 'supposed' to be strong, like prayer, love, faith, patience, unselfishness and humility.

Not coping with our own weakness can be very debilitating. It can lead us to spend hours going over and over some occasion when we think we've failed, to see how we could have done better. Or we may spend hours beforehand trying to ensure that we won't show up our lack of wisdom and understanding, or our incompetence. If we find our weaknesses and failures too difficult, we may refuse to face them at all, preferring to put all the blame on others when things go wrong.

It may be that we don't respond well to criticism, rejecting it or becoming angry, however lovingly it is given. Perhaps we become

discouraged or frustrated with ourselves, finding it hard to go on learning and trying again.
We may then refuse opportunities to do things,
afraid of being criticized or failing once more

All this can stem from ambivalent attitudes
toward God's grace, his free and unconditional giving that is the basis of all his dealings
with us. We know, at least in theory, that he
loves us infinitely, offering us limitless and
unconditional acceptance and forgiveness –
but we don't always find such grace easy.
Pride and fear collude against grace. Our pride
has difficulty with the fact that God does deal
with us on the basis of grace, while our fear
worries that he might not. Thus, our pride
says, 'I want to deserve God's favour. I need
to show that I have something to contribute.'
Our fear says, 'I know that I do not deserve
God's favour. I am afraid of being rejected
because I haven't got anything good enough to
contribute.'

Fortunately, God can cope very well with
our weakness, as Paul discovered. He writes,
'He [the Lord] said to me, "My grace is suffi-
cient for you, for power is made perfect in
weakness." So, I will boast all the more gladly
of my weaknesses, so that the power of Christ
may dwell in me … For whenever I am weak,
then I am strong' (2 Corinthians 12:9). This
passage is linked closely in my mind with John
15, where Jesus says, 'Apart from me you can

do nothing' (John 15:5). Coming to God empty-handed, with nothing to offer in terms of goodness or holiness, is an appropriate way to come – as one verse of the hymn 'Rock of Ages' puts it:

Nothing in my hand I bring,
Simply to thy cross I cling;
Naked, look to thee for dress;
Helpless, look to thee for grace ...

To be aware of our weakness can be a positive asset, because it leads us to depend on God, rather than on our own strength and cleverness.

Being a vicarage family with four children, we would sometimes experience some kind of irritation, argument or upset as we got ready for church on a Sunday morning. I was quite often one of the team available at the service for people who needed prayer for healing. If we'd had an upset or argument before going to church, I felt particularly unworthy of this task. I used to pray not only for God's forgiveness, but also that he would not allow my sin and weakness to hinder anyone else's healing. I was surprised at first that those times seemed more often than most to bring people peace and healing. It soon dawned on me that the very fact of admitting my weakness enabled God to use me more, because I had to cast myself on his mercy and grace. Thus, although the weakness was not in itself good, I could rejoice within it, because it led to blessing for others.

Loss of confidence, which sometimes accompanies a sense of weakness, can have a paralysing effect. We are tempted to think that if we cannot do things well, preferably perfectly, we shouldn't attempt them at all. This may seem quite logical when we apply it to ourselves – but we can clearly see how ridiculous it is when we apply it to other people. We can see many people, in public life and among our own friends and acquaintances, who aren't perfect and don't do things perfectly – but whose work and influence is very worthwhile none the less. God uses weak and imperfect people. In fact, there aren't any others available! I have found it helpful on occasion to remind myself of this.

We may be afraid that other people will despise or reject us because of our weaknesses. But, far from despising us, people are often helped by seeing that it is all right to be weak, to fail. We may actually encourage someone else by allowing them to see something of our own weakness.

It is good to remember that God knows and understands us completely. He made us and knows all our weaknesses, better than we know them ourselves. He doesn't expect more from us than we are able to give. The Psalmist puts it well: 'As a father has compassion for his children, so the Lord has compassion for those who fear him. For he knows how we were made; he remembers that we are dust' (Psalm 103:13-14). We may find it hard to accept ourselves, to love ourselves, to forgive ourselves – perhaps we even despise ourselves – but God does not despise us. We need to keep reminding ourselves of that fact over and over again, until we are sure of it deep in our being.

A few years ago, I had an experience that helped me to know in my heart, as well as in my head, that it is all right to be weak. I was away on a course, part of which involved a three-day retreat. On the second morning, although I had been given a Bible passage for meditation, I felt strongly that I wanted instead to make a horse's head out of modelling clay. I had done nothing similar since school-days, but I got the clay and began to shape a horse's head. After about 20 minutes I had a model which, while neither absolutely accurate nor an artistic masterpiece, was undoubtedly a horse's head and, to my eyes at least, one with a great deal of life and character to it. I washed my hands, put the model on the window-sill to dry and spent the afternoon looking at it, enjoying and delighting in it. It had something of me in it. Although it had idiosyncrasies and weaknesses, I even delighted in them, because they made my horse special, unique. When the person directing my retreat came to see me, she spent some time also gazing at my model and listening to me describing my feelings about making it and delighting in it. She compared my words with those of Julian of Norwich in her *Revelations of Divine Love*, her vision of the Lord holding 'everything that is made' in his hand like a hazelnut. Julian wrote, 'God made it, … God loves it and … God looks after it.' I was amazed by the comparison. I felt I had entered into something of how God feels about his creation, including some insight into how he may cope with what is less than perfect.

Four months later, I was feeling discouraged again about my weakness (physical weakness in this case), and also about the fact that I wasn't coping with it very well. My horse's head was on the mantelpiece and as I looked at it, I remembered my insights into God's attitudes towards our imperfections. This time I was looking from the creature's point of view, imagining the imperfect horse's head looking into the eyes of its creator, and I not only believed but felt that God's delight in me was not diminished by my weaknesses. If God accepts and loves me like that, I can accept and love myself.

I was also helped by reading a book called *Solitude* by the psychologist Anthony Storr. In it he talks about some of the world's most creative people – writers, thinkers and artists – who suffered various traumas of emotionally dysfunctional family life, or loss, bereavement and separation in childhood. These circumstances led to greater than normal periods of solitude, which could be seen as having caused emotional damage and weakness. Learning to cope with solitude, however, to value it and turn it to good use, actually resulted in artistic and philosophical works of genius which actually *required* long periods of solitude for their production. If these people had been healed of their 'weakness', and therefore had not valued solitude as much as they did, perhaps many works of genius would never have been created. So, on a lesser scale, it may be with our weaknesses: it is not only after they are healed that good can come. God can bring good out of the very weaknesses themselves.

If we are discouraged about our weaknesses, we have only two choices – unless we consider giving up completely on trying to serve God.

● We can ask God to work on our weaknesses first, before we offer ourselves in his service, until virtually no trace of them remains. The obvious disadvantage of this is that we may well run out of time before all our major weaknesses are dealt with! Even if we do not, we may miss many valuable opportunities on the way.

● We can get on with serving God now as best we can, asking him to heal and strengthen us as we go along. This is far better, and it is the way God deals with people throughout the Bible and Christian history. It is, therefore, a choice we can make positively and joyfully, confident that it is not God's second-best. It is how he wants us to proceed.

A couple of years ago I was struck by a phrase from the Bible that seemed to sum up very neatly the things God had been teaching me, bit by bit over the years, about my perfectionism. They were the words from Mark's Gospel where Jesus is defending the woman who had poured some expensive ointment over his head. He says, 'Let her alone ... She has done what she could' (Mark 14:6, 8). The words, 'she has done what she could', spoke very powerfully to me. Jesus was saying that he accepted and valued what the woman had done. Her critics thought she should have sold the ointment and used the money to help the poor. From some points of view you could argue that it would indeed have been better – the anointing was a luxury, whereas the poor lacked even basic necessities. The implication of Jesus' comment is that he appreciated what she *had* done, rather than looking to find some 'better' thing that she had not done. What mattered to him was that she had done what she could, and he valued the extravagant love that prompted her action.

The message to me of, 'She has done what she could', was, and still is, that God does not ask of me what I *cannot* give, but only what I *can*. This means that if all that I can manage to offer God is imperfect, because I am weak and imperfect, that is all right with him. He accepts it and is pleased. Might he even be ready to defend me against perfectionist critics (myself included), on the grounds that I have done what I could? He values the love and the cost to me that lie behind what I offer and do for him.

This struggle with weakness has been for me a struggle not only with my own weakness, but also with the weakness of the Church. I want the Church, local and global, to be strong, a good, successful set-up, something to which I am proud to belong, a community that really changes things and shows God to the world in all his glory, love and power. Instead I have sometimes felt afraid of looking foolish by belonging to a community that cannot deliver what it promises and does not practise what it preaches, but exhibits pettiness, feebleness and lack of love.

It is true that the Christian Church down the centuries has been a very powerful force for good, and the means by which millions of people have come to know God. But it has had some notoriously weak points too, and not every local church is effective in living and sharing the love of Christ. We have to learn to live with the Church and its weaknesses, as God himself does, and as we do with ourselves and our own weaknesses.

God seems to allow weakness in his people, partly to keep us humble, or in some cases to make us humble. Although we might want the Church to be strong and successful in its task of winning the world for God, it has never been exactly like that, even at the beginning. Paul wrote to one part of the early church, 'Consider your own call, brothers and sisters: not many of you were wise by human standards, not many were powerful, not many were of noble birth. But God chose what is low and despised in the world to shame the wise; God chose what is weak to shame the strong' (1 Corinthians 1:26-7). The Church is likely always to be like that, because most of those who join it are people who know their need of God, a need which the wise and the powerful do not necessarily realize.

In recent years, I have felt that God is calling me to give prayer a bigger place in my life, and I have tried to do that. One of the results is a greater realization of the feebleness of my praying. I still sense the call there, however, although I have nothing much to offer in response, except myself and my time, a sort of, 'Yes. I'll be there. I'll try. I'm sorry it is so feeble. Please help me.' For God, though, that is enough.

A prayer

Dear Lord, we fall so far short of what we would like to be and do. Thank you for forgiving and accepting us, not despising us, but even, it seems, delighting in us. Enable us to discern how to rejoice in weakness as an opportunity for your grace, while not becoming lazy or casual about our sin. Help us to accept and forgive ourselves as you do; through Jesus Christ, our Lord. Amen.

13

Will God ever give up on me?

Does God regard us as dispensable parts of some great machine? Will he discard us if he thinks we are no longer useful, or does he value us for ourselves always?

A few months after our third child was born, I looked in the mirror one day and I noticed a lump. Not a very big lump, but definitely noticeable. It was at the base of my neck, on the right. At first, I just felt a bit stunned by my discovery, but then my imagination began to run riot: I was convinced that it was cancer, that I would soon be quite ill and be dead in six months! And Graham would be left with three children under four years old. How would he cope? I was scared.

I visited the doctor, who said that it was a lump on my thyroid gland, fairly common in women of my age and usually nothing to worry about. Just to be on the safe side, he referred me to a surgeon. A few weeks later, I saw the surgeon, who said much the same thing: only about a 5 per cent chance of it being anything malignant, but best to take it out, just in case. So he put me on his waiting-list for surgery.

After a few months, I got a date for the operation, but two days beforehand it was cancelled because of a nurses' strike. I soon got another date for it and went into hospital on the day before, for the necessary examinations and tests. Alas, though, I woke up next morning with a sore throat, which meant I couldn't have the operation and had to be sent home.

I had prayed for healing several times and David Watson, a vicar with a powerful healing ministry, visited us one day, and he too prayed for my healing. We would all have preferred such healing to be direct, without the need for an operation – but we also recognized that the healing which comes through the skills of doctors and surgeons is equally from God. And the latter, it seemed, was going to be God's method in my case.

In due course, I was given a third date for the operation, and this time I actually had it. I had asked my GP to tell me the results of the tests on the lump. They were expected to be all clear, but I wanted to know for certain. A couple of weeks after the operation, there was a

ring at the front door – it was our GP who
brought good news that the lump had been
completely and successfully removed. But
there was bad news too: apparently the borderline between healthy and malignant cells is
rather fuzzy, and the cells of my lump were
just on the malignant side of this borderline. I
was, therefore, to take medication for the rest
of my life to suppress the thyroid gland and
thus make a recurrence less likely. The doctor
was as reassuring as he could be, but it was a
nasty shock all the same. I was going to have
to live with a degree of uncertainty for some
time.

Twenty-four years have passed since then,
with no recurrence – but at first I found the
uncertainty depressing. For several years, in
fact, whenever I experienced a new or
unknown pain, I wondered whether it was
cancer. Graham tried to comfort me: 'God will
only allow it if it is somehow for the best.' I
suppose he meant that a recurrence was
unlikely to be for the best, but I did not find
that very convincing, especially when I was
feeling unwell or a bit down. I would think
that, since I failed often as a Christian, as a
wife and as a mother (of, by then, four children), it could well be God's best plan to allow
me to disappear from the scene.

One evening, four or five years after the
operation, I had a sore throat, and these

thoughts were going through my mind yet again, when I suddenly had a sense of Jesus standing beside me and saying, 'But my best is to make the best of you.' Those words spoke right to the heart of my being; to God, I am not just a cog or a machine-part, to be replaced if I do not function well. I am someone God values so much that he will not only refuse to discard me, but make it a top priority to shape me into the very best that I can be!

For a moment I wondered whether I was deceiving myself – is God really like that? Does he really feel like that about me? Was the thought that had popped into my head merely my own wishful thinking, and not God speaking to me at all? I asked myself if the words 'My best is to make the best of you' are true to the God of the Bible. And it seemed to me that they are not only consistent with the God of the Bible, but actually epitomize God's attitude and action towards his people. For instance, he does not give up on Abraham, the liar (Genesis 20:2), Moses the murderer and coward (Exodus 2:11-15 and 4:13-14), David the adulterer (2 Samuel 11) or the nation of Israel when they repeatedly went after other gods (Hosea 11:1-4, 8-9). In fact, he made efforts to encourage them and bring them back to himself. He went out of his way, too, after the resurrection, to give to Peter, who had denied him three times, a new call and sense of purpose (John 21:15-19). Time and again in the Bible, God meets people who have failed him, or whose lives are in a mess – often a mess of their own making – and not only accepts and forgives them, but also restores their hope and sense of purpose.

It was very gracious of God to speak to me directly in order to bring home to my heart a message that had been staring me in the face from the pages of the Bible for years! I am particularly grateful to him for speaking that truth so deeply into me, that I have been able to hang on to it ever since. And it is not a promise for me alone: God never wants to give up on anyone. He always wants to take each of us on from wherever we are now, to be the best that we can be.

A prayer

Father, forgive us for the times when we think of you as less loving and less committed to us than you actually are. Help us to trust you and your goodwill towards us at all times. Enable us so to take this truth to heart and believe it deep in our being, that when hard times come, we shall be able to hang on and know that it is still true. May we trust you always to do the best for us, and to make the very best of us; in Jesus' name. Amen.

14

What can I do with my pain?

'I'm hurting, Lord!'
'And I'm here.'

'But I'm *really* hurting!'
'And I'm *really* here.'

'Lord, you don't understand how much I'm hurting!'
'And you don't understand how much I'm here.'

'I see, Lord. Your presence is enough for all my hurting. I need to let you come close, to be alongside me in my pain and share it with me.'
'Yes.'

This dialogue took place as I prayed one time when I was suffering not physical but emotional pain. What I believe the Lord was saying to me then was that, no matter what the depth and degree of my pain, he is more than a match for it. And that I have much more to learn about what his presence means, or can mean.

It is not that he promises to change the situation which is causing pain – although he does sometimes do that. It is, rather, that he is reminding me of his promise to all his people, 'I will never leave you, nor forsake you' (Hebrews 13:5). He will always be with me, alongside me, to help me. Knowing that can lessen emotional pain and distress, because having someone around who loves us and is committed to us always brings support and peace. When that someone is God himself, who knows and understands everything, including both our situation and our feelings, it is surely even more reassuring and comforting.

God does not reject or deny our thoughts, our feelings or our questions. He doesn't tell us that we shouldn't be asking the questions we are asking, that we shouldn't be thinking and feeling as we are. He may, in due course, lead us into better and more whole ways of asking, thinking and feeling – but he is ready, in the meantime, to stay with us, to love us and to help us.

At the end of Romans 8, Paul lists many disasters that might assail him – indeed, most of

them already had, at some time or other – but
then says that none of these things, 'nor anything else in all creation, will be able to sepa-
rate us from the love of God in Christ Jesus,
our Lord' (Romans 8:39). Christ's loving and
committed presence, which he promises us
always, is enough to see us through all painful
situations.

However, we do not always allow him to be
the help to us that he might be. Sometimes we
may perceive him as being over against us,
rather than alongside us to help. We see him
as, at least partly, the cause of our trouble,
because he has failed to prevent it, and we
may want to hit out at him, not invite him to
come closer. And sometimes we think he is
present, but more like an observer, watching to
see how we cope, rather than as the loving
friend he is, longing to be close and supportive
if we will let him. Or perhaps we think of him
as busy, with far more important concerns
than our distress. This makes God in our own
finite image, yet he is infinite and, without
lessening his attention to anything or anyone
else, able to give each one of us as much love
and attention as if we were the only one he had
to consider.

It is not just a question of God being around,
but of how close he is to us, to our inner being.
We want to know that he is really meeting
with us and dealing with us deeply, whether

or not we are fully conscious of what he is doing. Naturally, we prefer to be aware of his presence and of what he is doing with us, and he often works that way. But if we aren't aware of him, it doesn't mean that he is absent, or doing nothing. The quality and intensity of his presence are important to us, but these aren't always best measured by our awareness of them. From ordinary life we know that a patient is not conscious of the surgeon's presence and possibly life-saving activity during an operation. And sleeping children are blissfully unaware of all that their parents may be doing for them while they rest.

God is everywhere and knows everything. He is aware of aspects of ourselves which we do not necessarily understand: the automatic processes and functioning of our bodies, and what goes on in our subconscious minds and feelings. Thus, in a way, he is more present to us than we are to ourselves, always as fully present to us as it is possible to be, giving us his loving attention and understanding, deep inside us and alongside us. It is hard to put into words the completeness and intensity of his presence, but I have found it helpful to ponder the words he gave me, 'You don't understand how much I'm here.'

A prayer

Thank you, God, for wanting to be alongside us all the time, for choosing to share our pain and to help us. Teach us to recognize your presence and to let you come as close to us as possible. Enable us to trust you to be there, even when we are not aware of you, through Jesus Christ, our friend and Saviour. Amen.

15

Does Christianity really make a difference?

Much of what I have written is about inner struggles, finding a way through them with the Lord, and coming to terms with ourselves. I have written about these things because I have had to deal with them myself and have discovered that many others have to do the same. It is worth spending some time and attention on sorting them out. However, it has always seemed to me that, if following Jesus is really something worth giving our whole lives to, it must do more than enable a relatively small number of people to feel more comfortable with themselves and with life.

But is Christianity just one way among many of working with people's psychological make-up to enable them to feel better about themselves and about life? Or is it the truth about a God who has acted decisively in Jesus to deal with human sin and selfishness, and is still active to bring about healing and life-giving change in individual lives and in the world? Feeling better about ourselves is good, but the Christian Good News is far bigger than that. The call of the gospel to follow Jesus is not a call to a self-indulgent concentration on ourselves, but to loving him and working with him in his plan to change the world and give it a realistic hope. The world is in a mess, spoilt by sin, evil, suffering and death. It needs to be loved, forgiven, healed and set right. If Christianity cannot make a difference in these areas, it is no good.

How do we know whether it can make a difference or not? We shall have to look hardest at the people who have taken the Christian faith on board, the followers of Christ – that is, you, me and the rest of the Church. The people who give us the most reliable evidence of the difference Christ can make will be those who are most wholehearted and single-minded in their response to him. As G.K. Chesterton said, 'The Christian ideal has not been tried and found wanting. It has been found difficult; and left untried.'

What difference can we see in the lives of Christian people? Is there an increase of love, joy, peace and goodness, not only a sense of inner well-being, but an improvement in attitudes and behaviour? Does being Christian affect our lifestyle, our priorities and choices? Does it lead to greater love for God and a more active compassion for other people?

Merely asking these questions reminds us that we do not live out our faith as well as we could and should. We have to consider whether this is because God cannot or will not do what he has promised – or because we do not allow him to do so. God has given us freedom to choose whether or not we respond to him. He does not take back this freedom in order to force his will upon us.

If God cannot, or will not, put things right and establish his rule (the Kingdom of God), then the Christian message is not true. If the Christian message is true, then we are certain eventually to see what God is doing, even if we do not discern it all now. We should expect to recognize his activity when people are healed, prayers are answered, or peace and reconciliation come about.

Our individual inner peace is not unimportant, but the Christian faith claims to be much more than that. The Christian claim is that God has done something through Jesus that no one else has done or could possibly ever do, to put right the mess of human sin and selfishness in the world. If Christianity cannot, or does not, make a difference to that, what good is it? It would be no more than another religious commodity on the supermarket shelf. If the

Christian faith is no more than a way of making ourselves feel comfortable, it falls far short of what it claims to be. It wouldn't be worthless, but it wouldn't be a world-changing message to capture people's hearts and lives.

The questions, then, are, does Christianity really work, does it make a difference – and if so, how?

Christianity certainly works for many people in terms of offering a vision and purpose in life which is bigger than ourselves, and outward-looking, rather than focused on ourselves and our internal worries. In some of the earlier chapters we have looked at the way in which sorting out some of our internal worries actually moves us to become more God-centred, surrendering to his will and concentrating on giving love rather than getting it. Finding God's meaning for our lives leads us to grow in love – an outward-looking attitude. Our increasing faith and our willingness to hold God's gifts on an open hand make us more freely available for him to send in any direction he chooses.

Christianity makes a difference to those who commit themselves to Christ in trust: it transforms their lives. It does not remove all difficulties – in fact, sometimes it seems to increase them. But through the challenges and our wrestling with faith, God brings about good things: the peace of knowing that even

our worst sins are forgiven, the sense of worth
that comes from knowing that God cares about
us, the freedom from regrets in trusting God
to bring good out of everything, and the confidence to go on with him because he accepts
us in our weakness – these are just some of
the things already mentioned in previous
chapters.

Dealing with some of our inner worries – so
long as we do not spend longer on it than we
need to, or degenerate into navel-gazing – can
liberate us, enabling us to concentrate more on
God and other people. We become more open-
hearted and generous in spirit, more sensitive,
and able to help others. We are more willing to
pay the cost of working with God, to put right
what spoils his world and to build communities of compassion, justice and unity.

Christianity, when taken seriously, changes
individual lives for good. Not that Christians
are necessarily better than other people – but
they are generally better than they would have
been had they not been Christians. They do
find God's power transforming them: they
become inwardly more at ease and whole, and
they grow in concern and action for the well-
being of others.

Many Christians also testify that God
answers prayer. Circumstances change (sometimes remarkably), people cope better than
predicted and things turn out unexpectedly

well. People are helped and find healing – not merely emotional healing, which some may explain in psychological terms, but also sometimes physical healing. And this is not simply in individual lives, but on a much larger scale. The transition to multiracial elections and government in South Africa under Nelson Mandela is truly remarkable, as have been some of the moves towards peace in Northern Ireland. It is never possible to prove that anything is an answer to prayer – it may just be coincidence. But Archbishop William Temple once commented that when he stopped praying coincidences seemed to stop happening! We still see today something of the power of prayer to bring wholeness and goodness into situations – a power that was so characteristic of Jesus' earthly life 2,000 years ago. This is the Christian good news at work, making a difference. It is the beginning of the Kingdom of God, with the promise of more to come.

The irrefutable demonstration that Christianity makes a difference can only come after this life, when we shall see whether or not God really is there as Maker and Judge, whether our sins are forgiven through Christ and we are loved, accepted and welcomed into heaven as his friends, whether evil is fully and finally destroyed and God's rule is established for ever. In this life, the test is whether or not Christians actually experience a real and living relationship with God, who answers prayer and who is actively working for good in the world and in individual lives. Obviously we cannot prove these things beyond all shadow of doubt – but the evidence we have so far is enough to encourage us to go on. For now it is a journey of faith, with many mountains and molehills on the way, but we are travelling and working with God, trusting that one day we shall arrive and view with wonder the greatness of all that he has planned and done.

A prayer

Father, thank you for the scale, the wonder and complexity of all that you are doing. We cannot understand how you are everywhere, able to attend to everyone and everything at once. Small concerns do not have to compete with greater ones for your attention. Thank you for including us in your plans, for the difference you make in our lives as well as in the wider world. Teach us to recognize your hand at work, to grow in faith and wholeness, as we seek to love and serve you more and more; through Jesus Christ, our Lord. Amen.